Poland's
Gourmet Cuisine

This book is dedicated to the people of Poland who have shared the culture of their table with me.

Bernard Lussiana

Poland's Gourmet Cuisine

Bernard Lussiana

Mary Pinińska

Hippocrene Books, Inc.

Hippocrene Books, Inc. edition, 1999

Text
Mary Pinińska

Recipes
Bernard Lussiana

Photographs of dishes
Jarosław Madejski

Other photographs
*Lechosław Herz, Mariusz Jarymowicz
and Jarosław Madejski*

Graphic design
Paweł Kamiński

Cover design
Paweł Pasternak

Editor
Bożena Jagoszewska

ISBN 0-7818-0790-5

Printed by Białostockie Zakłady Graficzne

Contents

Meanwhile the centrepiece was changing scene,

And, stripped of snow, was now becoming green;

For as the summer warmth was slowly felt,

The froth of sugar ice began to melt,

And showed a basis hitherto concealed.

Another season's landscape was revealed,

And shone with verdant spring of every hue.

The crops appeared as if with yeast they grew,

And ears of saffron burst forth with gold,

And silver rye leaves started to unfold,

And buckwheat cunningly of chocolate wrought,

And orchards bloomed with pears and apples fraught.

Adam Mickiewicz, *Pan Tadeusz*

FOREWORD

It gives me great pleasure to write a foreword to this book, not only as the General Manager of Le Royal Meridien Bristol where, in our Malinowa Restaurant, you can find many of the dishes described over the following pages, but also as a member of an industry which strives to promote Poland and its many facets, from the warm, hospitable people, the music, the history, the country-side and the food.

Bernard Lussiana has been at Le Royal Meridien Bristol for over three years now and his parti-cular interpretation of Polish cuisine has become famous, not only in Warsaw, but with institutions, newspapers and magazines outside the country who have recognised his excellence in numerous awards and articles about his food.

Poland's Gourmet Cusine does, I feel, serve a dual purpose. For those born and bred in Poland, they will be able to read with pride a testimony to their culinary culture, their literature and their countryside which have endured so much and which is the source of inspiration for the recipes that follow. For those living abroad, I hope that indeed another landscape will be revealed and that having read this book they will understand a little more about Poland...

Bernie Gassenbauer

Warsaw 1998

NOTE TO THE READER

All recipes serve six unless otherwise stated. However, the quantities for ingredients listed in this book are for guidance only. As the cook, have the courage of your convictions, adapt according to your taste and let your personality develop along with the dish. Cooking should be a pleasure not a chore and the joy of creating should be balanced with the aim of feeding the souls of your guests and not just their stomachs.

"A man died and went to visit hell. He saw there a large table filled with all the culinary wonders of the world. On either side sat long rows of unhappy faces. He asked why, when in front of them there were such delicacies, the people looked so sad and were not eating. In answer, he was shown their forks, which were so long that it was impossible for people to feed themselves.

He went up to heaven and was surprised to see an identical table with the same abundance of delectable fare and the same impossibly long forks. However, the people who sat around the table radiated happiness and were eating. With great curiosity he watched to see how they had overcome the difficulty for they were using their long forks. Each one there was feeding his neighbour."

Enjoy these recipes and enjoy sharing them.

INTRODUCTION

Perhaps some explanation is required as to why a French chef's interpretation of Polish cuisine as seen in the recipes that follow is relevant in today's kitchen. It is not of course, the first time that a Frenchman has recorded his interest in Polish food. Guillaume de Beauplan, resident in Poland from 1630—1648, swelled the archives of Polish culinary history with his detailed observations of local customs and dishes. Edouard de Pomiane, with his gastronomic explorations of Poland, did the same earlier this century. No doubt, it will not be the last either, but it does come at a particular time in the development of the Polish kitchen.

Like most countries, Poland has a wealth of national dishes. The haggis of the Scottish, paella of the Spanish or goulash of the Hungarians are the pierogi, gołąbki or flaki of the Poles. So too, does Poland have a store of national ingredients — buckwheat, poppy seeds, carp, pike, beet, suckling pig, wild boar, horseradish and dill, to name just a few. These items are as much part of Poland's heritage as the music of Chopin or the poems of Norwid are in other spheres of the arts. But it is in the use of them that the nation's culinary art is formed.

Art, however, or creation by its very nature has to evolve. Fresh layers must be built on old foundations. Influences from across the centuries or the borders incorporated. Breaking new ground is what drives the artist on in his search to contribute a cultural brick in the slowly forming walls of time.

This century, repeated wars and decades of communism have proved catastrophic to the development of Poland's cuisine. Great literature can be fed by adversity, great cooking cannot. Instead of progression there has been regression. People ate what they could find and creativity was stifled by limitation. Lack of new culinary initiatives has meant that the traditional fare of yesteryear is more firmly embedded in the gastronomic consciousness of Poland than in many other countries across Europe. That, in itself, should be a cause for rejoicing. Poland has lost too much in the past to be careless with its heritage of the table. But whilst a rich culinary history is there to be drawn on by today's chefs, it is in their reinterpretation of familiar ingredients, their personal vision of the bounty now available, but for so long so scarce, that they create not just new dishes but a way forward. That is the relevance of Bernard Lussiana's recipes in the Polish kitchen of the 1990's.

Born in 1966 in Bourg-en-Bresse, France, Bernard knew from an early age what he wanted to do in life. Permeating his childhood was his family's love of food and the creativity within him was fuelled by the dishes made for him by his maternal grandmother, herself a cook in private service in Lyons. Bernard was twelve when his grandmother died, but his mother took on the role of tutor and continued to nurture the passion that had sparked so young.

After school and technical college Lussiana began a steady progression up the ladder in a number of gastronomic restaurants in France and Switzerland. In 1989 he joined L'Hermitage Ravet, a 2 star Michelin restaurant, rated 19/20 by Gault & Millau as Chef Tournant, going on to become Executive Sous-Chef in 1991. His years there were influential ones. Not only did he learn new techniques and increase his knowledge of food but there he came to recognise cuisine as an indivisible part of culture as a whole, a view which has marked his personal style. When he left it was because he was ready to strike out on his own.

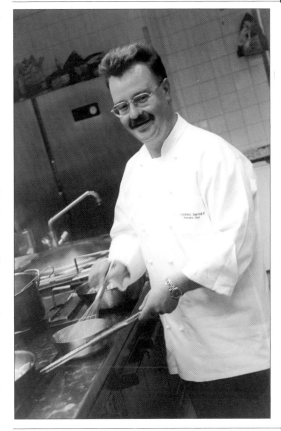

The challenge Lussiana was looking for was waiting for him on his arrival in Poland in 1995. From the fully developed culinary worlds of France and Switzerland, he revelled in the underdeveloped gastronomic landscape of Poland. He saw the untapped wealth of natural ingredients and applied his deep understanding of food to retain the spirit of the elements he wanted to work with, whilst interpreting them anew.

Arguably, it is easier for a foreigner, free of the weight of the nation's culinary history to select, with a fresh eye, those pillars on which a new kitchen can stand firm. But that is only possible if the soul and culture of the country have been absorbed, without which renovation becomes merely imposition.

Within his first year, Lussiana created culinary history when his recipe of *Braised rack of suckling pig with Żubrówka grass* won a silver medal for the Polish team at the First Regional Contest of European Flavours staged in France. Despite the fact that the aromatic qualities of the uniquely Polish bison grass had long been recognised and used in its flavouring of vodka, it had never before been combined with food. As Lussiana said, "It does not matter who is responsible for the recipe, but it is important that it has been recorded as an example of today's Polish kitchen."

Other indigenous Polish ingredients have been refashioned by Lussiana. Buckwheat, relegated for centuries to a side role, is used to encrust the juices of a fillet of pike-perch; poppy seeds encase pike. Carp and crayfish are rolled into "zrazy". Rustic pierogi are elevated by their filling of crab and accompaniment of a shellfish sauce; uszki are stuffed with rabbit and marjoram and surround a cumin emulsion. Cabbage leaves are wrapped around venison to produce a more sophisticated version of gołąbki. Beet leaves, before only found in botwinka, swaddle a ballotine of baby chicken and are dappled with a chłodnik sauce. Wieliczka salt forms a bed for a fillet of salmon. Bison grass is married with game, contrasted with turbot and even spikes the harlequin of three Polish vodkas. Śliwowica vodka flambées salmon trout and Pieprzówka vodka flavours bitki of

beef. Beets appear as a dessert their natural sweetness enhanced by a poaching in spice-infused syrup and a filling of saffron crème brûlée.

These are the raw materials that Lussiana works with. Applied to them are the tools of technique and a style, long matured to a point where it is recognisably his own. Hallmarks include the frequent partnering of water with field or forest; his love of working with fish — so well served here in Poland with produce from the clear Mazurian and Kashubian lakes and the country's many rivers; his zeal for the forests and what dwells within them and his constant inspiration from the seasons, especially that "season of mists and mellow fruitfulness", autumn.

All the recipes in this book are representative of Lussiana's kitchen, but among those that best reflect the multifaceted spirit of his cooking are: *Cream of kohlrabi soup flavoured with chives* for its natural simplicity; for the association of forest and water — *Turbot roasted with sunflower seeds, served with a bison grass sauce* or *Ceps filled with Mazurian crayfish; Escalopes of venison in a crust of hazelnuts, served with a wild rose fruit sauce* for its sense of autumn and feeling for the forest; *Roasted veal shank with savory and smoked garlic* for its knowledgeable combination of taste and flavour. *Pan-fried Dublin Bay prawns served in a crunchy cage with a flower emulsion* for its intangible lightness. *Dream around a rose* for its technical ability to create a variety of dishes based on one ingredient.

Just as the palette of an artist contains all the colours of a rainbow and more with which he can work his images, Lussiana's palette holds ingredients from Poland's fields and forests, rivers and lakes. It is the countryside which feeds his creative imagination and is the source of the emotion found in his dishes. Drawing on the deep respect he has for those ingredients and his perception of the spirit contained within them, Lussiana has used his skills to display the rich potential within the Polish kitchen and, as much as one man can, prepare the nation's culinary art for its natural journey onwards.

In more ways than one, the pages of a new chapter of Polish cooking lie before you...

There can be few restaurants which have a history stretching back nearly a hundred years and are still today at the forefront of innovative cuisine.

It was perhaps more the people than the food which made the Malinowa famous in the past, for as the restaurant of the Hotel Bristol it was the scene of many a state occasion. Its character fluctuating with the times as the history of the country moulded its clientele.

From the moment of its birth in 1901 the Malinowa was an immediate success, bringing in not only a healthy share of the hotel's profits but also renown as the city's finest restaurant. Memorable dinners, elegant dances and even the first New Year's Eve Ball to be held in a hotel filled its first decade of existence.

Those carefree years were sweet but short. Frivolity was replaced by World War I. The Malinowa

was requisitioned by the German army to serve war lunches. Respite between wars was brief. In 1920, during the Bolshevik War the restaurant was again requisitioned, this time by the Polish army.

But the clouds cleared. The Malinowa, under the expert guidance of Józef Jabłonowski the Maitre d'hotel of the Bristol entered a new epoch of splendour. The menus which have survived from this interwar period make as interesting a read as do the list of events held in the Malinowa and the Golden Book in which eminent guests penned their comments at the invitation of Jabłonowski.

On the menus, the vogue at the time for fashions French is represented alongside the national pride for things Polish. Dishes from both cultures were served to a range of guests as varied as Marshall Ferdinand Foch, Édouard Daladier; film stars Mary Pickford and Douglas Fairbanks; Stanisław Wojciechowski, President of Poland; Jabłoński, Mayor of Warsaw; leading figures from the worlds of art and music; the rich and the merely well-born.

The most famous event of those years though was a dinner in 1923, held by Piłsudski to announce his retirement from politics and recorded in memoirs of the time. "All the participants — more than two hundred then and very few now remember this moving farewell. The glow of the lights brightly reflected on the floors, in the mirrors and against the glass and silver of the Sala Malinowa in the Hotel Bristol."

In 1928 Ignacy Pade- rewski, the main sharehold- er of the Bristol since its founding, sold his stake. The new owners, the Bank Cu- krownictwa, authorised a complete renovation of the hotel's interior to make it the most up-to-date, elegant and fashionable hotel in Central Europe. The Malino- wa continued to flourish, a part of it under the new name of the Wojciech Kossak room. The artist Kossak, who had a studio at the top of the Bristol lived perma- nently beyond his means to the detriment of the Hotel who had difficulties extract- ing monies owed to them.

After a certain amount of pressure, Kossak gave eight of his paintings to the Bristol, in lieu of rent and they were hung in the Malinowa, prompting the change of name.

During the Second World War the Bristol, located in the middle of the German district, became **Nur fur Deutsche** (for Germans only). The restaurant was busier than ever serving up to 3000 meals a day to German officers on leave from the Eastern front and visiting high-ranking officials such as Hermann Göring. The staff in the Malinowa Restaurant kept their ears open and passed nuggets of useful information to the Polish Resistance. The staff in the Malinowa kitchens siphoned off up to twenty parcels of food a week from the German provisions to send to Poles in the prison camps.

The Bristol survived the Second World War, but not without damage. Public money was used to repair it, which according to the communists then gave them the justification to nationalise the hotel in 1948.

On December 21, 1949, the Malinowa Restaurant passed into history. Launched in its place, on the occasion that evening of the 70th birthday of Generalissimus J. Stalin was "Gospoda Ludowa." In due course the raspberry coloured walls were framed by bas-reliefs depicting scenes from the life of a peasant woman. The menus lost their "decadent" French influences and the waiters their tips, due to a stern phrase at the bottom of the carte: "Giving tips offends the dignity of the worker — therefore service is not included."

In the 1960's the reputation of cuisine at the Bristol was still high. Many state banquets were held there for visitors such as the German Chancellor Willy Brandt, the Shah of Iran, Reza Pahlavi and the French President, Charles de Gaulle. But already by the 1970's the one-time splendour of the Malinowa era lay threadbare.

With the opening of the Hotel Victoria in 1976, the Bristol was doomed. It struggled on for a few short years, without money from the state for maintenance and bereft of foreign V.I.P. guests who were now housed in the Victoria. In 1981 the hotel ground to a halt and the Bristol closed its doors after a rich history of eighty years.

The end was luckily merely an interval. In 1992 after a total renovation, the Malinowa, complete with its rightful name and elegant décor returned to its role as the fine dining restaurant of the beautifully restored Hotel Bristol.

Bernard Lussiana arrived as Head Chef of the Malinowa in the spring of 1995. Like an echo from its prewar past, the menus soon represented both the French culture from whence Lussiana had come and the Polish traditions that he absorbed.

This intertwining of different culinary worlds and the fresh interpretation of national cuisine produced a style unique in post-communist Warsaw, where "new" was represented by a flood of restaurants serving foreign food and "old" the unchanged Polish eateries with dated dishes.

Recognition for both the quality and creativity of food at the Malinowa has been wide. Locals view it as the best restaurant in Warsaw, the international food guides have been generous in their praise and culinary competitions unanimous in their verdicts.

As this book goes to press, Paweł Oszczyk from the Malinowa has just won a Silver medal at the Second Regional Contest of European Flavours held in France. His dish, created under Lussiana's supervision, of *Fillet of bison in a Żubrówka sauce, its brain cooked in a crust of clay and salt from Wieliczka, and a salad of its smoked tongue embedded in fresh pumpkin bread* competed against 43 other European regions.

To repeat, there can be few restaurants which have a history stretching back near on a hundred years and are still today at the forefront of innovative cuisine.

Recipes

Starters

Warm salad of pike perch seasoned with fresh herbs and slivers of smoked eel

•

Pan-fried Dublin Bay prawns served in a crunchy cage with a flower emulsion

•

Pierogi of crab and bigos

•

Fresh salmon smoked "à la minute" with herbs and spices, served with a beet
and sour cream sauce

•

Thin slices of fresh salmon trout flambéed with Śliwowica vodka

•

Ceps stuffed with Mazurian crayfish

•

Mille-feuille of "andruty" waffles and smoked fish mousse

•

Bouquet of salad and suckling pig ham braised in raspberry vinegar

•

Warm salad of venison fillet marinated with pine honey

•

Uszka of rabbit and marjoram, served with a cumin emulsion

•

Stew of veal tripe "Warsaw style"

•

Salad of smoked wild boar loin, roasted curd cheese and sweet and sour
forest blackberries

Warm salad
of pike perch seasoned with fresh herbs and slivers of smoked eel

EFFILOCHÉE DE SANDRE AUX HERBES FRAICHES ET COPEAUX D'ANGUILLE FUMÉE

1 ¹/₂ pounds pike perch fillets, without skin

  (if unarailable walleye perch can be used)

4 ¹/₄ ounces frozen smoked eel fillet, without skin

Salt, pepper

1 ¹/₂ cups assorted salad leaves

3 tablespoons lemon and olive oil dressing (see glossary)

For the marinade

2 tablespoons lemon juice

4 tablespoons extra virgin olive oil

1 teaspoon fresh marjoram, chopped finely

1 teaspoon fresh dill, chopped finely

1 teaspoon fresh parsley, chopped finely

³/₄ teaspoon fresh mint, chopped finely

³/₄ teaspoon fresh chives, chopped finely

For decoration

1 teaspoon fresh marjoram

1 teaspoon fresh dill

1 teaspoon fresh parsley

³/₄ teaspoon fresh mint

³/₄ teaspoon fresh chives

1   Marinate the pike perch in the lemon juice, olive oil and herbs for 1 ¹/₂ hours.

2   Carve the smoked eel into very thin slivers (it is easier to do this while the eel is still frozen).

3   Remove the pike perch from its marinade. Season it and steam it for 6 ¹/₂ minutes.

4   Wash and dry the salad. Arrange it on the individual plates and drizzle the lemon and olive oil dressing on top.

5   Carefully separate segments of the pike perch and arrange them on the plates. Scatter the slivers of smoked eel over the fish and salad.

6   Break the remaining herbs roughly between your fingers and scatter them over the salad. Serve warm.

Pan-fried Dublin Bay prawns served in a crunchy cage with a flower emulsion

PÔELÉE DE LANGOUSTINES EN CAGE, UNE ÉMULSION DE FLEURS

24 Dublin Bay prawns
  (2 ½ ounces each)
4 tablespoons olive oil

For the crunchy cage

³/₄ cup white flour
1 large egg
4 teaspoons elderflower syrup
¹/₄ teaspoon curry powder
¹/₄ teaspoon turmeric
¹/₄ teaspoon cardamom
¹/₄ teaspoon paprika
Salt

For the sauce

4 tablespoons rose water
1 ¹/₂ tablespoons white wine
3 tablespoons butter, chilled
  and diced

1 tablespoon lemon juice
2 teaspoons honey

Spaghetti of vegetables

2 tablespoons butter
¹/₂ cup zucchini and ¹/₂ cup carrots, cut
  into spaghetti-like strips and blanched

For decoration

Spices as used opposite
4 teaspoons *julienne* of rose petals

1. Preheat the oven to 225°F. Make the dough for the crunchy cage: sift the flour into a bowl. Make a well in the middle. Break in the egg and gradually incorporate it into the flour, adding the elderflower syrup, a pinch of salt and enough water to produce a smooth consistency. Leave the mixture to stand for 30 minutes.

2. Put the dough into a piping bag and using a small nozzle, pipe out onto greaseproof paper, very thin lines of dough. They should crisscross each other to produce the effect of a net. Sprinkle the spices over the "net" and bake in the oven until firm and crispy but not coloured. Cut carefully with a sharp knife into 12 triangles.

3. Clean the prawns and remove their intestinal tract by running a small knife along the top of the prawns and pulling it out. Pour the olive oil into a frying pan. When it is very hot quickly pan-fry the prawns. Remove them with a slotted spoon and reserve them. Deglaze the pan with the rose water and white wine. Whisk in the butter gradually, stirring constantly until you have a smooth emulsion. It is important that the butter is cold, if it is too soft it will melt too quickly and not emulsify. Finish the sauce by whisking in the lemon juice and honey and season.

4. In a frying pan, melt the butter and toss the vegetables in it. Remove and arrange a bed of them on each plate.

5. Put 4 prawns on top of each bed of vegetables and the net of dough like a cage around them. Surround each cage with a little sauce. Dust the edge of each plate with spices and decorate with the *julienne* of rose petals.

Pierogi
of crab and bigos

PIÉROGI DE CRABE ET BIGOS

Predating the existence of a Polish kitchen, pierogi *are thought to have originated in old Slavic folk cuisine. The name most probably comes from the Russian* pirogi, *derived from the verb* pirowat — *to feast. As this implies,* pierogi *were at one time feast-day fare, but after the introduction of Christianity they were often served on fast days, the number of which, some 200, gave ample scope to experiment with a variety of meatless fillings. To date,* pierogi *are one of the mainstays of the Polish kitchen but their role has never varied from that of rustic, home-cooked, simple, filling fare. Add crab to the traditional sauerkraut, however and a shellfish sauce and* pierogi *are at once elevated to fulfill a more sophisticated place on today's table.*

24

For the dough

4 cups white flour

4 large eggs

4 large egg yolks

3 tablespoons rape seed oil

2 teaspoons salt

3 ½ tablespoons hot water

1 large egg yolk, beaten, to seal the dough

For the stuffing

3 ½ tablespoons onions, diced

3 tablespoons butter

7 ounces oyster mushrooms, sliced

13 ounces sauerkraut, rinsed and dried

7 ounces meat and coral from 4 crabs
(spider crabs are preferable) poached in a *court
bouillon* (see glossary; reserve shells for the sauce)

1 teaspoon fresh thyme, chopped

3 ¼ cups heavy cream

Salt, pepper

2 teaspoons breadcrumbs

For the shellfish sauce

Shells of 4 crabs

⅔ cup *brunoise* of vegetables
(carrots, celeriac, onions; see glossary)

2 tablespoons butter

½ cup white wine

½ cup fish stock

2 cups heavy cream

1 *bouquet garni* (see glossary)

For decoration

6 green crabs

Fresh herbs

1   Prepare the dough: sift the flour into a large bowl. Make a well in the centre of it and gradually add eggs, yolks, oil and salt. Add the hot water and continue mixing until you have a smooth dough. Cover with plastic wrap and refrigerate for one hour.

2   Make the stuffing: pan-fry the onions in the butter. Add the mushrooms and let their juices evaporate. Stir in the sauerkraut and the crabmeat. Cook for 8 minutes. Add thyme and cream and cook for another 12 minutes. Season the stuffing. Stir in the breadcrumbs, spoon onto a metal tray and leave to cool.

3   Make the shellfish sauce: crush the crab shells. In a pan sweat the vegetables in the butter, without colouring. Add the crab shells and cook over a very low heat. Deglaze the pan with the white wine and fish stock. Add the cream and *bouquet garni* and bring to the boil. Reduce the heat to a minimum and leave it to cook slowly for 30 minutes. Strain and blend the sauce until smooth. Season.

4   Make the pierogi: roll out the dough very thinly (¹/₁₆ inch) and cut into circles of 3 ¼ inches. Put a spoon of stuffing in the middle of each circle, brush the edges of the dough with beaten egg yolk and fold over carefully, pinching them shut. Bring a large pot of water to the boil with salt and a dash of oil. Cook the pierogi in this for 8 minutes. Drain and arrange on the plates with a little sauce, serving the rest separately. Decorate each plate with one green crab and some fresh herbs.

Fresh salmon smoked "à la minute" with herbs and spices, served with a beet and sour cream sauce

SAUMON FUMÉ "MINUTE" AUX HERBES ET ÉPICES, UNE CRÈME AIGRE DE BETTERAVES ROUGES

1 1/2 pounds fillet of salmon, without skin

Olive oil

8 ounces assorted salad leaves

3 tablespoons olive oil and lemon dressing
  (see glossary)

3 tablespoons salmon caviar

For the pancakes

3/4 cup white flour

2 eggs

4 teaspoons butter, melted

1/3 cup milk

1 3/4 ounces smoked salmon, chopped

2 teaspoons chives

Salt, pepper

Herbs for smoking

1/3 cup dry grass

2 teaspoons bison grass

1 teaspoon cardamom

8 whole cloves

8 whole black peppercorns

1 tablespoon dried mushrooms

1 teaspoon juniper berries

For the sauce

3 1/2 tablespoons beet juice

1/2 cup heavy cream

1 tablespoon lemon juice

For decoration

Fresh herbs

1 Prepare the pancake batter: sift the flour into a bowl and make a well in the middle. Add the eggs and melted butter and slowly incorporate the flour. Add the milk gradually to avoid lumps. When the mixture has a smooth consistency, add the smoked salmon and chives. Season and leave to stand for 1 hour. Preheat the oven to 200°F.

2 In a coffee grinder or spice grinder, grind all the herbs for smoking and put to one side.

3 Cut the fillet of salmon into 18 fingerlike strips.

4 Make the pancakes: ladle about 2 tablespoons of the pancake batter into a very hot, greased frying pan. Tilt the pan as you do so to let the mixture roll and cover the whole surface. The pancakes should be extremely thin, almost transparent. Cook for 30 to 40 seconds, turn over with a spatula and cook for another 30 seconds. Repeat this process until you have 6 pancakes. Place each pancake into a tartlet mould and bake for 30 minutes until the pancakes are crispy and will hold the shape of the moulds. Remove from the oven, take the pancakes out of their moulds and reserve.

5 Cook the salmon: heat a frying pan over a medium flame until hot. Sprinkle the herbs for smoking into it. Brush the fingers of salmon with a little olive oil and put them on a metal rack. Stand this in the frying pan, cover it and let the salmon smoke for 7 to 8 minutes.

6 Make the sauce: whisk the beet juice into the cream. Add the lemon juice and season to taste.

7 Wash and dry the salad, toss it in the dressing and arrange a little inside each pancake. Sprinkle with salmon caviar.

8 Arrange 3 fingers of the smoked salmon, which should still be warm, on individual plates. Spoon a little of the sauce around and serve the rest separately. Sprinkle on a few freshly chopped herbs to decorate and serve immediately.

*T*hin slices of fresh salmon trout flambéed with Śliwowica vodka

ESCALOPINES DE TRUITE DE MER FLAMBÉES À LA VODKA ŚLIWOWICA

*Fish and vodka are traditional partners, but here
the combination is served on a plate. Śliwowica vodka
is used to marinate the salmon trout,
incorporated into the rosy plum granita and in the last act appears
again to flambée the finished dish before the guest, representing
the fundamental elements of fire and water.*

28

1 pound fillet salmon trout, with skin

6 slices bread

9 ounces assorted salad leaves

4 teaspoons lemon and olive oil dressing
   (see glossary)

3 ½ tablespoons Śliwowica vodka (70%)

For the marinade

4 tablespoons Śliwowica vodka (40%)

1 teaspoon sugar

1 tablespoon sea salt

2 teaspoons dill

4 tablespoons white wine

¼ teaspoon ground white pepper

For the rillettes

2 ½ ounces smoked sea trout

4 tablespoons butter

1 tablespoon lemon juice

For the granita

1 ¼ cups water

½ cup plum juice

3 tablespoons plus 1 teaspoon Śliwowica
   vodka (40%)

2 tablespoons sugar

1   Put the salmon trout into a shallow earthenware dish. Mix the ingredients for the marinade together and pour over the fish. Leave in refrigerator for 36 hours, turning from time to time to ensure that all the flesh is well marinated.

2   Make the *rillettes:* chop the smoked salmon trout and the butter together. Add lemon juice, season and reserve.

3   Make the granita: pour the water, plum juice and Śliwowica into a saucepan. Add the sugar and cook slowly until dissolved. Take off the heat and leave to cool. When cool pour into a container and freeze until just beginning to set. Remove and beat thoroughly. Replace until frozen. It should have a more granular texture than a sorbet.

4   Remove the salmon trout from its marinade, pat dry and slice into very thin escalopes.

5   Toast the bread and cut into triangles. On top of each triangle, spread a little *rillette*.

6   Curl the escalopes of salmon trout into the shape of a rose and place one on top of each triangle of toast.

7   Wash and dry the salad. Toss in the dressing and arrange a small amount on each plate. Put two triangles of toast on each plate.

8   Warm the vodka over a low heat (it is easier to flambée when it is warm). Spoon the granita into glasses and add to the plates.

9   Flambée the toasts with vodka in front of your guests.

Ceps stuffed with Mazurian crayfish

CHAPEAUX DE BOLETS FARCIS AUX ÉCREVISSES DE MAZURIE

This dish is inspired by Mazuria, the land of lakes and forests. Unspoiled and unpolluted, the forests abound with wildlife, their floors carpeted, according to the season, with wild mushrooms or blueberries or tiny fragrant wild strawberries. The translucent lakes host a multitude of fish and provide a perfect setting for crayfish hunts by torchlight on dusky evenings.

One of the most popular dishes in the Malinowa, crayfish are not new to the menu. Even in the communist times, when the Malinowa was rechristened "The Inn of the People", there were 3 versions of crayfish on the menu. Whether "the people" could afford them was another matter...

12 ceps (with the same size caps, approx.
7 ounces each)

1 ¹/₂ tablespoons butter

2 teaspoons fresh tarragon, chopped

For the stuffing

9 ounces fillet of pike-perch (or walleye perch)

2 large egg whites

24 crayfish (2 ounces each), cleaned,
with intestinal tract removed and poached
in *court bouillon* (reserve shells; see glossary)

1 cup heavy cream

Salt, pepper

2 teaspoons tarragon, chopped

For the sauce

18 crayfish carcasses

4 ¹/₂ tablespoons butter

²/₃ cup *mirepoix* of vegetables (carrots,
celeriac, onions; see glossary)

4 tablespoons white wine

5 tablespoons fish stock

1 ¹/₂ teaspoons dried bison grass

1 cup heavy cream

For decoration

Fresh herbs

6 crayfish carcasses

1   Prepare the ceps. Wipe the caps with a damp cloth and remove the gills from the underside to allow room for
the stuffing. Peel and slice the stems.

2   Prepare the stuffing: blend the pike perch with the egg whites and half of the poached crayfish. Add the cream.
Check and correct the seasoning. Chop the rest of the poached crayfish into pieces of ¹/₂ inch and mix into the
stuffing with the tarragon. Season the cep caps and fill them with the stuffing. Wrap them up in pairs in plastic
wrap and reserve.

3   Prepare the sauce: crush the crayfish carcasses and roll them in butter with the vegetables. Deglaze the pan with
the white wine and the fish stock. Add the bison grass and cream and cook the sauce slowly
for 30 minutes. Strain and blend the sauce.

4   Cook the filled cep caps in a steamer for 10 minutes.

5   Pan-fry the cep stems in butter and tarragon. Arrange a bed of this mixture on each plate.
Remove the cep caps from the steamer, separate them and top the pan-fried stems
with two caps per person.

6   Pour a touch of sauce onto the plates and decorate with fresh herbs and the reserved crayfish carcasses.

Mille-feuille of "andruty" waffles and smoked fish mousse

MILLEFEUILLE DE GAUFRETTES "ANDRUTY" ET MOUSSE DE POISSONS FUMÉS

10 ounces assorted salad leaves

2 tablespoons olive oil and lemon
  dressing (see glossary)

For the waffle batter

1 1/4 cups buckwheat flour

1 1/4 cups white flour

1 teaspoon baking powder

2 tablespoons poppy seeds

1/2 cup butter, melted

1 1/2 cups heavy cream

1 cup milk

Salt

For the smoked fish mousse

4 ounces smoked eel

4 ounces smoked trout

4 ounces smoked salmon

Juice of 1 lemon

1 cup heavy cream

2 teaspoons fresh dill, chopped

Salt, pepper

For decoration

2 tablespoons salmon caviar

Fresh herbs

> *Glory be to God for dappled things —*
> *For skies of couple-colour as a brinded cow*
> *For rose moles all in stipple upon trout that swim;*

Gerard Manley Hopkins, *Pied Beauty*

1   Prepare the batter for the waffles: mix together both types of flour, the baking powder, poppy seeds and melted butter. Gradually stir in the cream and then the milk. Leave the batter to stand for 6 hours.

2   Make the smoked fish mousse: take two-thirds of each of the smoked fish and blend them together with the lemon juice. Force the mixture through a fine sieve. Whip the cream and fold in to the blended smoked fish. Add dill and season to taste. Chop the remaining portion of smoked fish into cubes of 1/4 inch and stir these into the mousse.

3   Pour the batter into the waffle forms and cook. When ready, cut them into triangles of 3 inches.

4   Arrange the waffles like a triple sandwich, with one spoon of smoked fish mousse between each layer. You should end up with three layers of waffles. Decorate the top of each mille-feuille with a little salmon caviar and herbs.

5   Wash and dry the salad, toss it in the dressing and arrange a little on each plate beside the mille-feuille.

Bouquet of salad and suckling pig ham braised in raspberry vinegar

BOUQUET DE SALADES ET JAMBON DE COCHON DE LAIT CONFIT AU VINAIGRE DE FRAMBOISES

2 ½ pounds ham of suckling pig
   on the bone
Salt, pepper
2 tablespoons oil

For the sauce

¾ cup sugar
5 ¼ cups raspberry vinegar
¼ cup white wine
⅔ cup brown stock (see glossary)
2 bay leaves
3 cloves
Salt, pepper

For the salad

13 ounces assorted salad leaves
4 teaspoons raspberry vinegar
3 tablespoons sunflower oil

For decoration

2 ounces fresh raspberries
Fresh herbs

The forest children, shorter than the rest,
The hawthorn with the elder on his breast
And blackberry to the lips of raspberry pressed.

Adam Mickiewicz, *Pan Tadeusz*

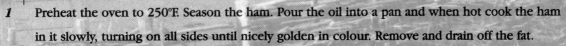

1   Preheat the oven to 250°F. Season the ham. Pour the oil into a pan and when hot cook the ham
    in it slowly, turning on all sides until nicely golden in colour. Remove and drain off the fat.

2   Melt the sugar in a heavy bottomed pan. Deglaze with the raspberry vinegar and white wine.
    Allow the mixture to reduce until the caramel has dissolved. Add the brown stock, bay leaves,
    cloves and seasoning. Infuse on a very low heat for 10 minutes. Add this sauce to the ham, cover
    and cook it in the oven until the meat is well glazed by the sauce, about 90 minutes. Remove the ham.
    Strain the sauce and skim the fat off it. Check the seasoning.

3   Wash and dry the salad. Dress it with the raspberry vinegar and the oil. Arrange a bouquet
    on each plate.

4   Carve the ham thinly and lay slices of it next to the salad. Spoon a touch of sauce on to the plates
    and serve the rest in a sauce boat. Decorate with fresh raspberries and herbs.

Warm salad of venison fillet marinated with pine honey

SALADE TIÈDE DE FILET DE CERF MARINÉ AU MIEL DE SAPIN

1 1/2 pounds venison fillet

2 tablespoons oil

1 pound salad leaves

For the marinade

1 1/2 cups vodka (40%)

1/2 cup pine honey

4 teaspoons pine needles

1 teaspoon juniper

1 teaspoon thyme

3/4 teaspoon pepper

5 bay leaves

Salt, pepper

For the dressing

3 tablespoons olive oil

4 teaspoons cider vinegar

4 teaspoons of marinade

For decoration

2 tablespoons pine nuts, roasted

Fresh herbs

> *The two things necessary to prepare*
> *A feast were joined: good cooking and good fare.*
>
> Adam Mickiewicz, *Pan Tadeusz*

1   Clean and trim the venison.

2   Prepare the marinade: pour the vodka into a saucepan, stir in the pine honey, pine needles and spices and warm until the honey has dissolved. Leave to cool.

3   Put the venison into a shallow earthenware dish and pour the marinade over it. Put in the refrigerator and leave for two days, turning the meat from time to ensure that it is all well marinated.

4   After two days remove the venison from its marinade, reserving the marinade, and pat dry.

5   Preheat the oven to 350°F. Bring the marinade to the boil, strain it and put to one side.

6   Heat the oil in a large casserole or roasting dish. Season the meat and when the oil is sufficiently hot, seal the venison quickly, turning on all sides. Finish cooking it in the oven until it is medium rare. As it will have been well marinated it does not need to cook for long.

7   Wash and dry the salad. Combine the ingredients for the dressing. Mix well and pour over the salad.

8   Carve the venison into thin slices and arrange on the plates with a bouquet of salad. Sprinkle on the pine nuts. Brush the meat with a little of the marinade and decorate with herbs.

Uszka of rabbit and marjoram, served with a cumin emulsion

USZKA DE LAPIN ET MARJOLAINE, UNE ÉMULSION DE CUMIN

For the dough

4 cups white flour
4 large eggs
4 large egg yolks
2 ½ tablespoons oil
2 teaspoons salt
¼ cup hot water

For the stuffing

½ rabbit (3 pounds whole)
2 cloves garlic
4 teaspoons fresh marjoram, chopped
4 tablespoons olive oil
Salt, pepper

White stock

4 cups water
Bones of the rabbit
1 cup onions, chopped
1 cup carrots, chopped
½ cup leeks, chopped
⅓ cup celeriac, chopped
1 *bouquet garni* (see glossary)

For the emulsion

White stock
1 ¼ cups heavy cream
1 teaspoon cumin
4 tablespoons butter, chilled and diced
1 tablespoon lemon juice

1   Prepare the dough for the *uszka*: sift the flour into a bowl. Make a well in the middle and add the eggs, egg yolks, oil and salt. Gradually add the hot water mixing everything together with your hands to form a soft, pliable dough. Knead and shape into a ball. Wrap with plastic wrap and reserve in the refrigerator for 4 hours.

2   Make the stuffing: bone the rabbit, keeping the bones for the stock and chop the meat very fine. Crush the garlic and add to the meat along with the marjoram and olive oil. Season to taste and reserve.

3   Prepare the white stock: pour the water into a pan and add the bones, vegetables and *bouquet garni*. Bring the water to the boil and allow to reduce to ¾ cup. Strain it. Make the sauce: pour the strained stock into a saucepan with the cream and cumin and cook slowly for 15 minutes.

4   Remove the dough from the refrigerator and roll out as thinly as possible on a lightly floured wooden board. Cut with a square cutter into squares of 2 ½ inches. On each square place a teaspoon of the stuffing. Wet the edges of the dough with water and fold over to form a triangle. Pinch the edges together firmly. Wet the ends of the dough with a little water and turn them inward, pinching them together to form *uszka*. Cook the *uszka* in boiling water until they float to the surface.

5   Finish the emulsion by gradually whisking in the butter and the lemon juice to achieve a smooth and glossy consistency.

6   Remove the *uszka*, drain thoroughly and arrange on the plates with the emulsion in the middle.

Stew
of veal tripe "Warsaw style"

MITONNÉE DE TRIPES À LA MODE DE VARSOVIE

4 1/2 tablespoons butter

1/3 cup carrots, cubed

1/3 cup onions, cubed

1/3 cup celeriac, cubed

1/3 cup leeks, cubed

2 pounds tripe, blanched
and sliced

2 teaspoons garlic, crushed

Salt, pepper

4 teaspoons dill

2 cups white wine

2 bay leaves

Cloves

For the choux pastry

3/4 cup water

5 tablespoons butter

1 cup white flour

3 large eggs

2/3 cup bone marrow

3 tablespoons fresh dill, chopped

1/2 cup white vinegar

1 Preheat the oven to 275°F. Melt the butter in a heavy bottomed pan and roll the vegetables in it.

Add the tripe, garlic and let it simmer for 15 minutes. Add 4 teaspoons of dill. Deglaze with the white wine.

Cover the pan and cook it in the oven for 3 hours.

2 Make the choux pastry: put the butter in the water and bring to the boil. When it has melted, tip in the flour all

at once and beat it with a wooden spoon for five minutes over a medium flame, until the mixture is smooth

and forms a ball in the centre of the pan. Remove from the heat and add the eggs, one by one, mixing constantly

until the dough has a glossy sheen. Allow to cool. Blend the marrow and add to the choux pastry with

4 teaspoons of chopped dill. Boil 1 quart of water with 4 tablespoons of the vinegar and salt to taste.

Form quenelles (dumplings) out of the marrow and choux pastry (there should be 18 in all) and drop these

into the boiling water. Poach them gently for 8 to 10 minutes, until doubled in size.

3 Remove the tripe from the oven. Season to taste. Add a dash of vinegar and 2 teaspoons of dill.

4 Spoon the tripe into six hot soup plates. Add three quenelles to each and the remaining 5 teaspoons dill.

Salad of smoked wild boar loin, roasted curd cheese and sweet and sour forest blackberries

SALADE DE LONGE DE SANGLIER FUMÉE, PERLES DE TWARÓG RÔTIES ET AIGRE DOUX DE MÛRES

"She had been walking to the table carrying a tray of egg-yolk candies when she first felt his hot gaze burning her skin. She turned her head, and her eyes met Pedro's. It was then she understood how dough feels when it is plunged into boiling oil. The heat that invaded her body was so real that she was afraid she would start to bubble — her face, her stomach, her heart, her breasts — like batter, and unable to endure his gaze she lowered her eyes and hastily crossed the room."

Laura Esquivel, *Like Water for Chocolate*

1 pound smoked wild boar loin

13 ounces curd cheese

2 teaspoons fresh marjoram, chopped

1 large egg white

For the batter

½ cup white flour

½ cup potato starch

2 teaspoons baking powder

Carbonated mineral water

For the sauce

½ cup sugar

¾ cup white vinegar

½ teaspoon mustard seeds

5 ounces (¾ cup) blackberries

For the salad

1 pound assorted salad leaves

4 teaspoons raspberry vinegar

2 tablespoons rape seed oil

Salt, pepper

For decoration

2 ounces (¼ cup) blackberries

Fresh herbs

1 Prepare the batter: mix the flour, starch and baking powder and add enough mineral water to produce a smooth consistency. Leave to stand for two hours.

2 Meanwhile make the sauce: in a heavy bottomed pan, heat the sugar very slowly until dark brown in colour. Deglaze with the vinegar. Add the mustard seeds and reduce until the liquid is syrupy in consistency (it is ready when it coats the back of a metal spoon). Add the blackberries and allow the sauce to return to the boil. Remove from the heat and leave the sauce to cool.

3 Carve the smoked wild boar loin into wafer thin slices.

4 Mix the curd cheese with the marjoram and form the mixture into 6 balls. Beat the egg white until it forms stiff peaks and fold into the batter. Roll the curd cheese balls in the batter until well coated and deep-fry them.

5 Wash and dry the salad. Make a dressing with the raspberry vinegar, rape seed oil and season to taste. Dress the salad and arrange a bouquet of salad leaves in the middle of each plate.

6 Cut each ball of curd cheese slightly open on top and arrange on the bouquet of salad twisted open so that the curd cheese is visible inside. Arrange slices of wild boar loin around the salad. Decorate the plates with a touch of sweet and sour blackberry sauce. Serve the rest in a sauce boat. Garnish each plate with a few blackberries and some fresh herbs.

Soups

Soup of sturgeon fins

•

Cream of kohlrabi soup, flavoured with chives

•

Barley consommé served with quenelles of smoked game

•

Tatry Mountain soup

Quand on se gorge d'un potage

Succulent comme un consommé

Si notre corps en est charmé

Notre ame l'est bien davantage

Paul Scarron

Soup
of sturgeon fins

SOUPE D'AILERONS D'ESTURGEON

Delicate and exotic, this soup is representative in two ways of Lussiana's kitchen. First, in its use of sturgeon fins it shows his creativity with all parts of a product. Second, in marrying the sturgeon soup with strips of buckwheat blinis a connection is made between water and ground — a recurrent theme in Lussiana's dishes.

Fins of one sturgeon

4 ¼ ounces sturgeon belly

4 tablespoons butter

²/₃ cup *brunoise* of vegetables (carrots, onions, celeriac; see glossary)

²/₃ cup white part of leeks, sliced

2 teaspoons smoked garlic

¹/₃ cup dry white wine

1 tablespoon fresh vesiga (marrow of sturgeon), chopped

2 teaspoons marjoram

Salt, pepper

1 ²/₃ cup heavy cream

4 egg yolks

For the buckwheat blinis

1 cup warm milk

2 teaspoons fresh yeast

1 cup buckwheat flour

2 tablespoons butter

2 large eggs yolks

Salt

2 large egg whites

Oil for frying

For decoration

2 teaspoons fresh dill, chopped

Optional decoration: a small *vol-au-vent* case filled with caviar

1   Chop the fins and belly of the sturgeon coarsely. In a heavy bottomed pan, melt the butter and sweat the vegetables and leeks until soft but not coloured. Add the fins and belly of the sturgeon and the smoked garlic. Simmer until all the liquid has evaporated. Deglaze the pan with the white wine. Add the fresh vesiga, marjoram, seasoning and 1 ¹/₃ cups of the cream and simmer on a low heat for 1 ¹/₄ hours.

2   Meanwhile prepare the blinis: pour the warm milk into a bowl and sprinkle the yeast onto the surface. Leave the bowl in a warm place for 15 minutes or until the mixture is frothy. Sift ¹/₂ cup of the flour into a large mixing bowl and gradually add the yeast mixture. Beat to a smooth batter. Cover the bowl with a clean cloth and leave to rise in a warm place for 30 minutes or until doubled in volume. Melt the butter and allow to cool slightly. Gradually add the remaining ¹/₂ cup flour to the risen batter, then the melted butter, the egg yolks and a pinch of salt. Beat the mixture until smooth. Cover the batter again and leave to double again in volume for 40 minutes. Whisk the egg whites until they stand in soft peaks and fold them into the risen batter. Heat a little oil in a heavy frying pan over high heat. Ladle a little of the batter into the pan, tilting the pan as you do so, so that the batter covers the whole surface. Cook the blinis for about 1 minute on each side or until they are golden brown. Reserve.

3   Remove the soup from the heat, strain it and return it to the saucepan. In a mixing bowl beat the egg yolks with the remaining ¹/₃ cup cream. When well mixed, whisk into the soup, do not bring back to the boil. Season.

4   Cut the blinis into fine strips. Scatter them into the soup bowls and pour in the soup. Sprinkle a little chopped dill onto each bowl of soup or top with caviar and serve.

Cream of kohlrabi soup, flavoured with chives

CRÈME DE COLRAVE ET CIBOULETTE

*An excellent source of vitamin c, kohlrabi, some say, came to Europe from Asia
with Attila the Hun. Chives, native to Europe were one of the seventy herbs listed by the
Emperor Charlemagne in 812 A.D. in the inventory of his garden.
These ancient ingredients, which have held a place in the Polish kitchen
for generations are here combined according to Escoffier's
dictum: "Fâites simple".*

6 purple kohlrabi (1 ⅓ pounds each)

1 potato, peeled and diced

½ cup onion, diced

3 ½ ounces leeks, diced

3 tablespoons butter

2 ½ cups white chicken stock (see glossary)

¾ cup heavy cream

Salt, pepper

2 tablespoons chives, chopped

... Into a magical dish
I shall throw my own soul.

Maria Pawlikowska-Jasnorzewska,
Różowa magia

1   Cut the tops and leaves off the kohlrabi, reserving the tops. Hollow out the flesh of each kohlrabi, taking care not to damage the skins. Reserve the kohlrabi shells. Dice the flesh. Sweat the potato, onion, leeks and kohlrabi flesh in the butter for 5 minutes. Cover with chicken stock and simmer slowly for 40 minutes.

2   Blend the soup in a mixer, add the cream. Check and correct the seasoning and at the last minute stir in the chives.

3   Pour the soup into the kohlrabi shells, replace their lids and serve immediately.

Barley consommé served with quenelles of smoked game

CONSOMMÉ D'ORGE PERLÉ ET MOUSSE DE GIBIER FUMÉ

*The earliest recorded recipe for soup written by the Roman epicurean Apicius
who lived in the first century, was for barley soup.
Barley was one of the first grains to be cultivated. It was grown by the ancient Egyptians
and used as a bread grain by the ancient Romans and Greeks. The Roman gladiators
were fed on barley. The Greeks treated it as a symbol of fertility.
In Poland, barley has long been associated with soup in the form of krupnik.
In this autumnal consommé are elements of both field and forest.*

$^{1}/_{2}$ cup pearl barley, soaked overnight in cold
water

For the game stock

6 pounds game bones (elk or venison)

2 tablespoons sunflower oil

2 cups *mirepoix* of vegetables (onions, carrots,
celeriac; see glossary)

2 tablespoons tomato paste

10 cups (2 $^{1}/_{2}$ quarts) water

1 bouquet garni (see glossary)

3 teaspoons tarragon

Salt, pepper

For the clarification

6 large egg whites

$^{1}/_{2}$ cup *brunoise* of vegetables (carrots, onions,
celeriac; see glossary)

10 ounces beef, sliced thinly

3 tablespoons chopped herbs

$^{1}/_{2}$ cup ice cubes

For the quenelles

3 $^{1}/_{4}$ ounces smoked venison loin

2 large egg whites

$^{1}/_{3}$ cup heavy cream

1 teaspoon tarragon, chopped

Salt, pepper

1   Preheat the oven to 350°F. Prepare the game stock: in the oven roast the bones, having sprinkled them
with the oil, until they are golden in colour. Add the vegetables and tomato paste. Turn the oven
down to 250°F and cook for another hour.

3   Remove the bones and vegetables and put them in a saucepan. Pour the cold water into the saucepan, add
the *bouquet garni* and seasoning and bring to the boil. Cook uncovered on a very low heat for 3 hours.
Strain and allow the stock to cool.

4   Clarify the stock: mix the egg whites, *brunoise* of vegetables, beef, herbs and ice cubes. Whisk into the stock
and reheat to simmering point, but do not allow it to boil. Simmer until a crust forms on the surface. Make
a hole in the crust with a ladle, where the bubbling is strongest, this will prevent a build up of heat and
the stock boiling over.

5   Take the pan off the heat and leave to rest for a few minutes. Pour the clear *consommé* through a fine sieve lined
with a damp piece of muslin. Leave to cool. This can be prepared the day before and refrigerated until needed.

6   Cook the pearl barley in one quart of water until tender. Strain it.

7   Blend the venison and force it through a fine muslin-lined sieve into a bowl set over ice. Add the egg whites, cream,
tarragon and seasoning and mix to a smooth paste. On a lightly floured surface divide the mixture into 18 oval
shapes. Bring the *consommé* almost to boiling point. Drop the quenelles into it and poach for 6 to 7 minutes.

8   Ladle the *consommé* into the soup bowls. Add a few spoonfuls of pearl barley and 3 quenelles to each bowl.

Tatry Mountain soup

SOUPE DES MONTAGNES DU TERTRE

Mountainous regions the world over have their own warming specialities of nourishing soups to stave off the chill of winter. This one draws its inspiration from the Tatra Mountains. Winter there is a fairy-tale world, with the tinkling bells of the horse-drawn sledges, echoing from valley to valley, the only sound to break the snow-muffled silence.

5 ½ ounces smoked wild boar bacon

2 ounces pork fat

3 tablespoons onions, cubed

½ cup celeriac, cubed

½ cup carrots cubed

1 cup potatoes, diced

4 ½ cups water

⅓ cup white beans

1 cup white cabbage, cut into 2 inch cubes

2 teaspoons marjoram

Salt, pepper

⅓ cup peas

½ cup whipped heavy cream

2 teaspoons fresh parsley, chopped

> *All excellent and homely cured they were*
> *Smoked in the chimney over juniper.*
>
> Adam Mickiewicz, *Pan Tadeusz*

1   Cut the wild boar bacon into strips. Melt the pork fat in a heavy bottomed saucepan, add the onion, celeriac, carrots and bacon and sweat slowly for about 5 minutes.

2   Add the potatoes and pour in the water. Add the white beans, cabbage and marjoram. Cook on a low heat for 1 hour 20 minutes. Check and correct seasoning.

3   Add the peas and cook for a further 10 minutes. Ladle into the soup plates, top with a spoon of whipped cream and sprinkle with chopped parsley.

Fish dishes

Delicate stew of perch fillet, chanterelles and ceps flavoured with marjoram

•

Pike fillet in a crust of poppy seeds, served with a nettle sauce

•

Fillet of cod stuffed with ceps, served with a nutmeg scented juice

•

Goulash of European catfish and eel, flavoured with paprika

•

Fillet of tench "Toruń style," flavoured with gingerbread

•

Fillet of salmon in a crust of Wieliczka salt, served with an emulsion
of olive oil and parsley juice

•

Zrazy of carp and crayfish, served with a red wine sauce, on a bed of vegetable tagliatelle

•

Fillet of pike-perch in a crust of buckwheat, served with a dill sauce

•

Delicate stew of crayfish, calf's head and feet

•

Mille-feuille of king prawns and pumpkin chutney cake

•

Fillet of osetr sturgeon stuffed with its own caviar, served with a Żubrówka sabayon

•

Turbot roasted with sunflower seeds, served with a bison grass sauce

Delicate stew
of perch fillet, chanterelles and ceps flavoured with marjoram

MARMITE DE PERCHES, CHANTERELLES ET BOLETS EN INFUSION DE MARJOLAINE

Flavours from Poland's forests and lakes fill produce from their fields. Nut brown ceps and golden-yellow chanterelles with their apricotlike aroma balance the sweet fleshed perch in a harmony of delicacy. The addition of marjoram, so long used in the Polish kitchen, gives body and depth to the dish but its subtle flavour does not dominate the whole.

6 kohlrabi (7 ounces each)

10 ounces chanterelles

10 ounces ceps

1 pound perch fillet, without skin

5 tablespoons olive oil

1 tablespoon onion, chopped

3/4 cup milk

2 tablespoons fresh marjoram, chopped

Salt, pepper

For decoration

Fresh marjoram, chopped

1 Cut the tops off the kohlrabi and carefully scoop out the flesh inside, with a small spoon, into little balls, making sure you do not damage the skin. Bring some salted water to the boil and cook the balls of kohlrabi in it until tender. Remove and reserve. In the same water poach the hollowed out kohlrabi skins and tops.

2 Clean the chanterelles and ceps and cut them into slices. Cut the perch fillets into cubes of 1 inch.

3 Pan-fry the mushrooms in half the olive oil. Add the onions and cook until softened. Strain the juice from the mushroom mixture into the milk and in a separate saucepan bring this to the boil. Reduce by half. Add the marjoram and cook slowly on a very low heat, uncovered, for 15 minutes.

4 Pan-fry the perch in the remaining olive oil. Mix with the mushrooms and onions. Season to taste and spoon into the hollow kohlrabi shells. Into each pour a little of the marjoram-infused sauce and replace the tops.

5 Put the kohlrabi shells on the plates. Around each one place some kohlrabi balls and pour the remaining sauce around them. Decorate with a little fresh marjoram.

Pike fillet
in a crust of poppy seeds,
served with a nettle sauce

PAVÉ DE BROCHET EN CROÛTE DE PAVOT ET ÉMULSION D'ORTIES

The pike is sealed with a layer of blue-black poppy seeds. An essential ingredient
in the Polish kitchen, poppy seeds are synonymous with cakes and pastries. In a fresh interpretation of their role, they are used here to enhance the sweetness of the firm-fleshed pike.
The culinary properties of nettles have been explored from the earliest times,
with some results more successful than others. The Frisian writer, Verdun,
commenting on Polish vodka in 1672 wrote: "The finest vodka is made
from rye and the worst is made from nettles." The sauce for this pike, though,
is one of the successes.

1 ³/₄ pounds pike fillet, without skin or bones

2 tablespoons white flour

1 large egg, beaten

4 ounces poppy seeds

2 ¹/₂ tablespoons clarified butter
(see glossary)

2 teaspoons fresh thyme

For the sabayon

¹/₂ cup young nettle leaves

3 large egg yolks

¹/₂ cup white wine

4 tablespoons olive oil

Salt, pepper

For the garnish

³/₄ pound celery sticks, cut into lozenges
and blanched, with leaves reserved

2 tablespoons butter

> *It seems as if a swarm of butterflies*
> *With fluttering wings has settled on their stems*
> *And glitters with a rainbow flash of gems,*
> *With so great brilliance do the poppies blaze;*
>
> Adam Mickiewicz, *Pan Tadeusz*

1 Preheat the oven to 325°F. Cut the pike fillet into six equal medallions. Sift the flour onto a board and roll the pieces of pike in it, making sure they are evenly coated. Shake gently to remove excess flour. Brush each pike medallion with a little beaten egg and dip them in the poppy seeds to form a crust on both sides.

2 Blanch the nettle leaves for 30 seconds in boiling water. Remove and plunge them into a bowl of cold water and ice to refresh them. Strain and dry them. Put into a blender and reduce them to a very thin puree.

3 Pan-fry the portions of pike quickly on both sides in a hot pan with the clarified butter. Chop the thyme, sprinkle it over the pike and finish cooking them in the oven for 5 minutes.

4 Make a sabayon: put the egg yolks and white wine into a glass bowl and set this over a pan of just simmering water (the bottom of the bowl should not touch the water). Whisk continuously until the mixture has expanded and has the consistency of lightly whipped cream. Gradually trickle in the olive oil, whisking all the time. Add seasoning and at the last minute the nettle puree (it will lose its colour if kept too long in the sabayon).

5 Roll the chopped celery in butter and season to taste. Lightly fry the celery leaves. Arrange a bed of celery on each plate. Place the pike medallions on top and a touch of sabayon around them. Decorate with fried celery leaves and serve.

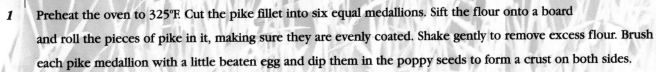

Fillet of cod stuffed with ceps, served with a nutmeg scented juice

DOS DE CABILLAUD FARCI AUX BOLETS, UN JUS MUSCADÉ

Cod has the image of a somewhat unexciting fish — perhaps because of its cheapness
and easy availability compared to other fish. It has though, had its influence on the history
of the world with some claiming that the European colonisation of North America
was provoked by the large shoals of cod on that side of the Atlantic. In previous
centuries dried and salted cod were a significant trade and even today remain
much eaten in Italy, Spain and Portugal.

Poland's cod come from the Baltic and their firm flesh and full flavour make them an ideal
fish to serve as below, wrapped in bacon, stuffed with ceps — the pride of Polish
mushrooms - and accompanied by a honey and nutmeg scented juice.

6 ounces smoked bacon

1 pound cod fillet without skin,
    middle portions only

2 tablespoons flour

3 tablespoons clarified butter (see glossary)

1 sprig fresh thyme

For the stuffing

14 ounces ceps, cleaned with a damp cloth

1 ½ tablespoons butter

2 tablespoons fresh parsley and chives, chopped

Salt, pepper

½ cup heavy cream

2 teaspoons breadcrumbs

1 large egg, beaten

For the sauce

⅓ cup white wine

1 teaspoon ground nutmeg

2 teaspoons honey

¾ cup brown stock (see glossary)

For the garnish

3 ounces cep heads, cut into
    slices of ¼ inch

4 tablespoons butter

10 ounces iceberg lettuce

For decoration

Fresh herbs

1   Preheat the oven to 325°F.

2   Make the stuffing: chop the ceps, heads and stalks, into cubes of ¼ inch. Heat a pan, melt 1 ½ tablespoons of butter in it and pan-fry the cep cubes. Season and add fresh herbs. When the liquid has evaporated, add the cream and the breadcrumbs and cook for 3—4 minutes. Off the heat mix the egg in thoroughly. Put to one side.

3   Cut the bacon into thin slices. Slice the sides of the cod fillets so as to make a pocket inside the fish. Fill these with the cep cube mixture. Season and wrap a slice of bacon around each portion of fish. Tie them with string. Sprinkle the flour over the cod parcels and pan-fry in the clarified butter until golden in colour. Add the thyme and finish cooking in the oven for 10 minutes, basting continously. Remove the fillets of fish and reserve. Skim off the fat from the pan.

4   Make the sauce: deglaze the pan with the white wine. Add the nutmeg and honey and reduce the sauce by half. Add the brown stock and allow it to infuse for 10—15 minutes. Strain the sauce and check the seasoning.

5   Make the garnish: Pan-fry the sliced cep caps in half the butter and reserve. Chop the lettuce into cubes and fry them quickly in the remaining butter. They should remain crunchy.

6   Put a bed of lettuce on each plate. Remove the string from the cod fillets and cut them into slices (there should be 12 in all). Arrange on the lettuce. Decorate with the sliced ceps. Pour a little nutmeg sauce around and serve the rest in a sauce boat. Garnish with fresh chopped herbs and serve.

*G*oulash
of European catfish
and eel, flavoured with paprika

GOULASH DE SILURE ET ANGUILLE AU PAPRIKA

1 ¼ pounds European catfish fillets, without skin and bones

7 ounces smoked eel fillets, without skin and bones

6 pumpkins (7 ounces each)

4 teaspoons sunflower oil

2 tablespoons onions, chopped

³/₄ cup red peppers, cut into *julienne* sticks (see glossary)

1 tablespoon tomato paste

²/₃ cup white wine

¹/₂ cup heavy cream

2 ¹/₂ teaspoons ground paprika

Salt, pepper

¹/₃ cup pickling onions

1 ¹/₂ tablespoons butter

2 teaspoons sugar

For decoration

Chopped, fresh herbs

1   Preheat the oven to 350°F.

2   Cut the catfish and eel into finger-sized portions.

3   Cut the heads off the pumpkins, reserving them, and carefully scoop out the seeds, taking care
    not to make a hole in the skins.

4   Pan-fry the catfish in hot sunflower oil. Remove the catfish and reserve it. In the same pan, fry the onions and red
    peppers. Add the tomato paste and deglaze with the white wine. Add the cream, paprika and seasoning and allow
    the sauce to reduce by half. Add the catfish and eel to the sauce and continue to cook for a further 5—7 minutes.

5   Put the pickling onions into a pan with the butter and sugar. Pour in enough water to come up level
    with the onions. Cover with a piece of greaseproof paper and cook until all the water has been absorbed.

6   Fill the pumpkins with the fish goulash and place both them and the pumpkin tops separately, in the oven for 12 minutes.

7   Arrange the pumpkins on the plates. Mix the onions and peppers into the fish goulash, decorate with fresh
    herbs, cover the pumpkins with their tops and serve.

Fillet of tench "Toruń style," flavoured with gingerbread

GOUJONETTES DE TANCHES AU PAIN D'ÉPICES

The old-fashioned sweet festive bread of Central Europe has a special connection
with the city of Toruń which, linked by the Vistula
to the Baltic Sea, was on the spice route.
It was there that the idea of adding spices to the traditional Slavonic
honey cake was born and a whole gingerbread "industry" came into existence,
with the variety of shapes and pictorial embossments turning the food into
an art form. Gingerbread has been favoured as a suitable partner to fish in
the classic Polish sour-sweet sauce for many a decade. Tench, like roach or bream
is from the same family as the carp.

64

1 ¾ pounds tench fillet,
   without skin

3 ½ ounces field mushrooms,
   sliced

2 tablespoons shallots, sliced

For the sauce

1 ¼ cup fish stock

1 ¼ cup heavy cream

4 ounces of gingerbread
(see recipe page 122)

2 ½ tablespoons butter

2 tablespoons lemon juice

Salt, pepper

For the garnish

2 ½ tablespoons butter

1 ½ pounds iceberg lettuce,
   chopped

For decoration

Fresh herbs

> *The best things in Poland are a liqueur from Gdańsk, gingerbread from Toruń, a maiden from Cracow and a shoe from Warsaw.*
>
> Old Polish Proverb

1   Preheat the oven to 400°F. Remove the bones from the fillets of tench with tweezers. Slice the fish into *goujonettes* of 2 ½ x ½ inch.

2   Bring the fish stock to the boil, add the cream and crumble the gingerbread into it. Reduce the sauce by two-thirds. Whisk in the butter, lemon juice and seasoning. In an ovenproof dish, arrange the sliced mushrooms, shallots and the tench. Pour the warm sauce over them. Cook in the oven for 7 minutes. Remove the tench and the mushrooms. Blend the sauce and season to taste.

3   Melt the butter in a hot pan and quickly toss the lettuce in it, keeping it crunchy. Arrange a bed of lettuce on each plate, put the tench and the mushrooms on top. Pour the sauce around, and decorate with fresh herbs.

Fillet of salmon in a crust of Wieliczka salt, served with an emulsion of olive oil and parsley juice

PAVÉ DE SAUMON AU SEL DE WIELICZKA, UNE ÉMULSION D'HUILE D'OLIVE ET JUS DE PERSIL

Poland has been rich in salt for many hundreds of years, with the salt mine of Wieliczka, near Cracow, being justifiably the most famous. Dating back to the 13th century there is a legend that the salt was miraculously brought from Hungary to Poland by the Blessed Kinga. Kinga apparently asked, before her arranged marriage to the Polish Bolesław the Chaste, what things were needed in Poland. On hearing of the lack of salt, Kinga traveled to the Hungarian salt mine of Marmarosz and threw her engagement ring into it. After their wedding, Kinga went to Wieliczka and there indicated a spot that should be excavated. Up came a large piece of rock salt in which was embedded her engagement ring. It is the only salt mine in the world to have been actively worked from the Middle Ages to the present day.

66

10 ounces coarse Wieliczka salt

5 ounces salmon fillet per person

2 tablespoons clarified butter
(see glossary)

For the emulsion

$^1/_2$ cup salmon or fish stock

$^1/_4$ cup heavy cream

2 tablespoons white wine vinegar

$^1/_2$ cup olive oil

7 ounces flat parsley

Salt, pepper

For the garnish

10 ounces black radish

2 tablespoons lemon juice

$^1/_4$ cup olive oil

1 $^1/_2$ tablespoons fresh parsley,
chopped

1   Preheat the oven to 225°F. Boil the fish stock, cream and vinegar together until it has reduced by a quarter.
Slowly dribble in the olive oil, whisking continuously until the sauce begins to thicken to a consistency
that coats the back of a spoon. Chop the parsley roughly and place in a juice extractor. Extract the juice and
whisk it into the sauce. Leave in a warm place for 5 to 10 minutes to allow the flavours to develop. Season to taste.

2   Prepare six mounds of salt on a baking tray and flatten to accommodate the fillets of salmon. Skin the salmon
and place the skin, scales downward, onto the salt. Return the salmon fillets to their skin and gather
the salt around them so they are encased. Brush the top of each fillet with clarified butter.
Put into the oven for 8 minutes.

3   Chop the black radish into *julienne* strips. Blanch them in boiling water, drain and toss them in a pan
over medium heat in lemon juice, olive oil, salt, pepper and a sprinkling of chopped parsley.

4   When the salmon is moist and pale but just cooked through, brush off the salt and remove the fish from
the baking tray. Arrange a bed of black radish on each plate, place the fillets of salmon on top and spoon a little
of the emulsion around.

Zrazy of carp and crayfish, served with a red wine sauce, on a bed of vegetable tagliatelle

ZRAZY DE CARPE ET ÉCREVISSES AU VIN ROUGE, TAGLIATELLES DE LEGUMES

*Classic Polish zrazy are often made with beef, but Lussiana in his quest
for a fresh interpretation of ancient customs utilises two typical Polish ingredients
to produce a fish and seafood variation on the theme.
Carp hold a special place amongst the fish of Poland and are traditional fare
on Christmas Eve. The first fish ever to be farmed, they have been
bred in Poland since the 13th century.
Crayfish, which are vanishing across much of Europe as the lakes
become more and more polluted, still thrive in abundance
in the crystal clear blue lakes of Mazuria.*

2 pounds carp fillet, without skin

For the stuffing

8 ounces salmon fillet
3 large egg whites
1 cup heavy cream
10 ounces crayfish meat, half cut
   into salpicon (see glossary)
Salt, pepper
3 1/2 ounces smoked bacon,
   cut into 6 very thin slices
2 tablespoons olive oil

For the sauce

4 cups red wine
2 bay leaves
Pinch of thyme
Pinch of marjoram
1 teaspoon shallot, diced
1 teaspoon honey
3 1/2 tablespoons butter
1/4 cup heavy cream

Tagliatelle of vegetables

1/2 cup carrots
1/2 cup celeriac
1/2 cup zucchini skin
1 1/2 tablespoons butter

For decoration

Chopped fresh herbs

1   Preheat the oven to 300°F.

2   Cut the carp fillets into thin escalopes approximately 1/4 inch thick. Remove bones and beat them out to a regular shape.

3   Prepare the stuffing: blend the salmon (this always works better if it is very cold), add the egg whites and then gradually blend in the cream. Season the mixture, add the salpicon of crayfish meat and put to one side.

4   Prepare the sauce: pour the red wine into a saucepan with the herbs, shallots and honey.
When it comes to the boil, flambée it to remove any acidity (see glossary). Reduce to 1/2 cup.
Delicately whisk in the butter and cream. Check the seasoning.

5   Take one square of aluminium foil per person. Brush it with a touch of olive oil and season it. Put the fillets of carp onto the foil squares, making a rectangle of approximately 6 inches. Put an equal amount of stuffing onto each portion of carp. Put the rest of the crayfish meat into the middle and roll it up carefully. Wrap a strip of bacon around each carp parcel. Fold over the aluminium foil so it completely encloses the fish. In a hot pan, greased with a little olive oil, seal the foil parcels. Remove and finish cooking in the oven for 15 minutes.

6   Chop the vegetables into tagliatelle-like strips. Melt the butter in a frying pan and quickly toss the vegetables in it.

7   Arrange a bed of vegetables on the centre of each plate, alternating the colours. Slice the zrazy and place 4 portions per person on top of the vegetables. On either side of the zrazy and vegetables trickle a little sauce, serving the rest separately. Decorate with fresh herbs.

Fillet of pike-perch in a crust of buckwheat, served with a dill sauce

FILET DE SANDRE EN CROÛTE DE SARRASIN, UN JUS À L'ANETH

*Pike-perch, buckwheat, dill and beet; the threads of old Polish cuisine are
here rewoven to form a dish intrinsic in spirit to the national kitchen. Buckwheat,
consistently popular since pagan times has, however, always been relegated to
a supporting role on the plate. In this recipe it moves to lead under the spotlight
as a double act with the pike-perch, whose juices it encases with a crisp,
nutty flavoured crust. A culinary symphony from Poland's fields and lakes.*

70

3 pounds pike-perch (or walleye
   perch) fillets, without skin

3 $^1/_2$ tablespoons clarified butter
   (see glossary)

For the buckwheat crust

3 $^2/_3$ cups water

$^1/_2$ teaspoon gingerbread spices

1 bay leaf

Pinch of thyme

Salt, pepper

2 cups buckwheat grains

5 tablespoons buckwheat flour

For the sauce

$^1/_2$ cup pike-perch fish stock

3 cups brown chicken stock
   (see glossary)

5 tablespoons dill

4 tablespoons butter

$^1/_2$ teaspoon sugar

Salt, pepper

For the garnish

1 pound beet, cut into *julienne* strips
   (see glossary)

4 teaspoons dill

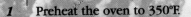

1   Preheat the oven to 350°F.

2   Prepare the buckwheat crust: bring 2 $^2/_3$ cups water to the boil. Add the spices, herbs and seasoning.
Add the buckwheat grains and cook slowly until all liquid has been absorbed. Reserve. Bring to the boil
the remaining water with the buckwheat flour. As soon as it has dissolved, add to the buckwheat grains
and mix together thoroughly. Leave to cool.

3   Cut the fish into 6 equal portions. Season them and press on the top and bottom of each one
a thin crust of buckwheat. Pan-fry the fish carefully on both sides in the clarified butter. As soon as the
buckwheat crust is lightly coloured, remove from the pan and finish cooking in the oven for 6 minutes.

4   Prepare the sauce: in a saucepan reduce the fish and chicken stocks to a good consistency.
Blend the dill with the butter and sugar and whisk in gradually to the stocks. Check the seasoning.

5   Slice the fish and arrange on the plates with a bouquet of *julienne* beets in the centre.
Pour a little sauce around the fish and decorate with the remaining dill.

Delicate
stew of crayfish, calf's head and feet

ÉTOUFFÉE D'ÉCREVISSES, TÊTE ET PIEDS DE VEAU

1 calf's head

4 calf's feet

2 ½ cups *mirepoix* of vegetables
(see glossary)

bouquet garni (see glossary)

1 cup leeks, chopped
(green part only)

Salt, pepper

½ cup white vinegar

36 crayfish (3 ounces each) poached

For the sauce

1 ¼ cups *brunoise* of vegetables
(see glossary)

2 ½ tablespoons butter

2 tablespoons winiak (or cognac)

½ cup white wine

¾ cup heavy cream

1 sprig rosemary

1 ¼ pounds leeks (white part only)

2 ½ tablespoons butter

2 ½ tablespoons sugar

For the dough

½ cup flour

1 large egg white

4 teaspoons sesame seeds

For decoration

Chopped fresh herbs

1   Blanch the calf's head and feet for 5 minutes. Remove and rinse with fresh water. Put in a saucepan and cover with cold water. Add the *mirepoix* of vegetables, *bouquet garni*, green leeks, seasoning and vinegar. Bring to the boil and cook slowly, uncovered, for 3 hours.

2   Remove the meat from 30 of the crayfish. Crush the carcasses. Preheat the oven to 275°F.

3   Prepare the sauce: roll the *brunoise* of vegetables in the butter. Add the crayfish carcasses and simmer for 10 minutes. Pour in the winiak and flambée, add the wine, cream and rosemary and infuse for 20 minutes. Strain and season.

4   For the dough: mix the flour with egg white and a drop of water. Onto greaseproof paper spoon the dough into six very thin rings of 3 inches. Sprinkle with sesame seeds and cook in the oven for 6—10 minutes.

5   Remove the calf's head and feet and flake the meat.

6   Slice the white leeks into rings of ¼ inch and toss in the butter. Add the sugar. Add water to just cover the leeks. Cook until tender. Season.

7   Add the meat to the leeks and a touch of sauce to bind it. Divide the mixture into 6 portions. Press each portion into a 3 inch round mould. Invert onto separate plates, removing the mould. Top the mixture with the pastry rounds. Decorate with a crayfish. Spoon the sauce around and garnish with fresh herbs.

Mille-feuille of king prawns and pumpkin chutney cake

MILLEFEUILLE DE CREVETTES ROYALES ET CAKE AU CHUTNEY DE POTIRON

A tower of contrasting textures, flavours and colours. Juicy king prawns are pan-fried, split open and wedged between layers of spice-infused pumpkin chutney cake to form a chain of differing tastes for the eater.

5 ounces (³/₄ cup) wild rice

¹/₃ cup olive oil

36 king prawns, without heads
   (approx. 1 ounce each),
   with intestinal tract removed

3 tablespoons white wine

For the pumpkin chutney

4 tablespoons white wine vinegar

8 ounces honey

¹/₂ ounce small chili

1 teaspoon mustard seeds

1 teaspoon cardamom seeds

¹/₂ bay leaf

¹/₂ teaspoon cloves

10 ounces pumpkin, peeled
   and cut into ³/₄ inch dice

For the cake

1 ²/₃ cups flour

2 teaspoons baking powder

3 large eggs

¹/₂ cup olive oil

4 ounces pumpkin chutney (see above)

For the sauce

1 ¹/₄ cups fish stock

²/₃ cup heavy cream

2 teaspoons honey

¹/₂ teaspoon curry powder

2 tablespoons apple juice

2 tablespoons lemon juice

Salt, pepper

3 tablespoons butter, chilled
   and diced

For decoration

Curry powder

Fresh herbs

1   **The day before:** make the pumpkin chutney cake. First prepare the chutney: bring the vinegar, honey and
    spices to the boil. Add the pumpkin and cook on a very low heat for 3—4 hours until the pumpkin is transparent.
    Take off the heat, leave to cool, strain and reserve.

2   Preheat the oven to 300°F. Make the cake: mix together the flour and baking powder. Stir in the eggs, one by one
    and mix in the olive oil. Carefully fold in 4 ounces of the pumpkin chutney. Pour the dough into a cake tin
    (10 x 4 inches) lined with greaseproof paper. Let it rest for 20 minutes and then put it in the oven for 30 minutes.
    Remove the cake from its tin and leave it to cool on a wire rack. Reserve in the refrigerator for 24 hours.

3   **On serving day:** bring the wild rice to the boil in a pan of salted water and cook until tender. Drain well
    and put to one side.

4   Cut the cake into thin slices of ¹/₄ inch. Cut out of these, with a 3 inch round cutter, 18 circles of cake.

5   Make the sauce: put the fish stock, cream, honey, curry, apple and lemon juice into a saucepan
    over a medium heat and reduce to a smooth consistency.

6   Pour the olive oil into a frying pan and when very hot quickly pan-fry the king prawns. Remove them with
    a slotted spoon and deglaze the pan with the white wine to dissolve the caramelised juices which have formed on
    the bottom of the pan. Add these juices to the sauce. Blend the sauce, strain it and check the seasoning. Return the
    sauce to a pan and finally whisk in the cold, diced butter, little by little until the sauce has a velvety consistency.

7   Put the circles of cake in a warm oven for a few minutes to heat up. Slice 24 of the prawns in half, lengthwise.

8   Assemble the mille-feuille: start with a layer of cake then two king prawns and a little wild rice, then another
    layer of cake topped by two king prawn halves and some wild rice and so on, finishing with a layer of cake.

9   Arrange the mille-feuille on individual plates. Divide the remaining 12 prawns into two per plate and put them beside
    the mille-feuille. Pour a little sauce around and decorate with a sprinkling of curry powder and some fresh herbs.

Fillet of osetr sturgeon stuffed with its own caviar, served with a Żubrówka sabayon

FILET D'ESTURGEON OSCIÈTRE FARCI DE SON CAVIAR ET SABAYON À LA ŻUBRÓWKA

*"A tear of Żubrówka could do Monsieur no harm. It's well known
to be very good for the kidneys.
We have just received a consignment from Poland."
"It tastes divine," said Isabel, "It's like mother's milk, I've never tasted anything
so good.. it smells of freshly mown hay and spring flowers, of thyme
and lavender, and it's soft on the palate and so comfortable,
it's like listening to music by moonlight."*
W. Somerset Maugham, *The Razor's Edge*

6 osetr sturgeon fillets, 5 ounces each
   trimmed and skinned

6 ounces osetr caviar

2 ½ tablespoons clarified butter
   (see glossary)

Salt, pepper

For the garnish

1 ¾ pounds chicory

2 tablespoons lemon juice

1 ½ tablespoons olive oil

Salt, pepper

For the sabayon

4 large egg yolks

⅓ cup white wine

2 tablespoons Żubrówka vodka

1 tablespoon lemon juice

Salt, pepper

3 ½ tablespoons clarified butter, melted

For decoration

Red rose petals

Fresh herbs

1   With a sharp carving knife, make a slit in the side of each sturgeon fillet, creating a pocket. Fill these
    with the caviar and carefully press the sides of the fish together to ensure that the caviar is well enclosed.
    Put the sturgeon on a wire rack and brush with clarified butter. Season and leave for 30 minutes.

2   Start the garnish: chop the chicory into large pieces at an angle. Discard the heart which is bitter. Sprinkle
    the lemon juice over it to prevent discolouration. Preheat the oven to 225°F.

3   Make the sabayon: in a bowl, whisk the egg yolks with the white wine until the mixture has expanded
    in volume and become light and foamy. Set the bowl in a *bain-marie* (see glossary), making sure that the water
    in the pan beneath it does not boil but is hot enough to gradually heat the sabayon. Whisk vigorously and
    continuously for about 5 minutes over a constant temperature. The sabayon should become firmer and have the
    consistency of lightly whipped cream. Add the vodka, lemon juice, seasoning and whisk in the clarified butter.

4   Pan-fry the chicory in olive oil, season and reserve.

5   Put the sturgeon in the oven for 14 minutes. Cooking at such a low temperature ensures that the sturgeon
    remains juicy and absorbs the flavour of the caviar. When the fish is cooked, the caviar should be just warmed
    through. Cut the fillets of sturgeon in half and arrange on a bed of chicory in such a way as to display the caviar
    inside them. Pour a little sabayon on the plate around the fish and serve the rest in a sauce boat.

6   Chop the rose petals into *julienne* sticks (see glossary). Decorate the plate with some fresh herbs
    and add to each a little *julienne* of roses for colour.

Turbot
roasted with sunflower seeds, served with a bison grass sauce

TURBOT RÔTI AUX GRAINES DE TOURNESOL, UN JUS À L'HERBE DE BISON

6 turbot fillets (5 ounces each)
   without skin
1 tablespoon flour
1 large egg
1 ½ tablespoons oil
2 ½ tablespoons sunflower seeds,
   chopped coarsely
Salt, pepper
1 ½ tablespoons clarified butter
   (see glossary)
1 sprig thyme
2 blades bison grass, chopped

For the sauce

2 teaspoons bison grass
⅓ cup brown stock (see glossary)
2 teaspoons dandelion flower jelly
   (see glossary)

4 tablespoons white wine
½ cup fish stock
2 tablespoons butter, chilled and diced

For the garnish

2 pounds spinach
2 tablespoons butter
3 tablespoons water

For decoration

Blades of bison grass and sunflowers

And like the moon amid the starry maze
With flaming countenance the round sunflower
Pursues the westering sun from hour to hour.

Adam Mickiewicz, *Pan Tadeusz*

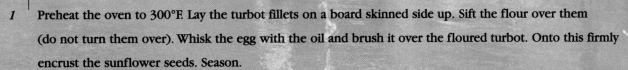

1   Preheat the oven to 300°F. Lay the turbot fillets on a board skinned side up. Sift the flour over them (do not turn them over). Whisk the egg with the oil and brush it over the floured turbot. Onto this firmly encrust the sunflower seeds. Season.

2   Start preparations for the sauce: infuse the bison grass in the brown stock with the dandelion flower jelly on a very low heat for 10 minutes.

3   In a hot pan melt the clarified butter and seal the turbot on the side which is encrusted with sunflower seeds. Turn the heat down and add the thyme and 2 chopped blades of bison grass. Finish cooking it in the oven for 7—8 minutes, basting regularly.

4   Make the garnish: wash the spinach thoroughly and dry it. Melt the butter in a pan and gently toss the spinach in it, adding a little water. Season.

5   Remove the turbot from the oven and take it out of the pan. Deglaze the pan with the white wine and fish stock and let it reduce. Add the infused brown stock and cook for a few minutes more. Strain the sauce and season. Return to the pan and whisk in the chilled, diced butter.

6   Put a bed of spinach onto each plate. Arrange the fillets of turbot on top and pour a little sauce around, serving the rest in a sauce boat. Decorate with a few blades of bison grass and some sunflowers and serve.

The Białowieża Forest

> *"The wild hop wreathed upon the currant bush;*
>
> *The service tree with shepherdess's blush;*
>
> *The hazel like a maenad clad with shapes*
>
> *Of thyruses and nut brown pearls like grapes.*
>
> *The forest children shorter than the rest,*
>
> *The hawthorn with the elder on his breast*
>
> *And blackberry to the lips of raspberry pressed...*
>
> *The trees and bushes joined their leafy hands*
>
> *Like men and girls preparing for a dance*
>
> *Around a married couple. Midst the host*
>
> *Of forest trees stood forth the pair that most*
>
> *Excel in slenderness and lovely hue,*
>
> *The darling silver birch and her spouse true,*
>
> *The hornbeam...;*

Adam Mickiewicz, *Pan Tadeusz*

When Adam Mickiewicz immortalised the great primeval forests of Białowieża in his epic, *Pan Tadeusz*, at the beginning of the 19th century, it was a crowning of the laurels. Already renowned across Europe for centuries as a spectacular hunting ground, with a wealth of game and in places a near impenetrable wilderness which added to the excitement of the chase, the forest, never cleared, had stood defiant against the march of time.

Playground to the kings, from the Jagiellionans and before that to the electors of Saxony, it was during the reign of Stanisław August (1764—1795) that the forest, perceived with "enlightened" eyes, was first respected as the unique ecological treasure it was. Animals such as the bison, elk and lynx, traditionally preserved for royal hunting parties, became protected and the pursuit of nature replaced that of sport.

At the end of the 18th century Białowieża fell into Russian hands as a result of the Partitions. At the beginning of the 19th century, the Napeolonic armies briefly reclaimed it for the Poles under the Duchy of Warsaw and the forest itself was the scene of fighting in the late Spring of 1812 as the Grand Armée pushed onwards into Russia, frightening even:

> *"The bearded bison in his mossy lair.*
> *Trembled, and bristled up his shaggy hair*
> *Half standing and upon his hind legs raised*
> *He shook his hoary beard, and saw amazed*
> *The glittering sparks that in the brushwood fell.."*

Despite the changes in ownership, an interest in nature and forestry was established firmly enough across national borders for Białowieża to become the subject of serious study. The man the Russians appointed to the task, Juliusz von

Brincken, was a German by origin and an experienced forester by profession. Even though von Brincken drew up plans for his masters to turn the wilderness of Białowieża into a source of economic prosperity with ideas for timber plantations and trees graded according to age and size, he also fell in love with the very charms that on paper he was struggling to discipline. The romantic in him recorded with pleasure the 815 rings on a fallen linden tree. The naturalist in him tracked the number of bison dwelling in the forest in 1828 to 732. He set out to refute the views of earlier, eminent, natural historians, among others the Swedish botanist, Carolus Linnaeus (1707—1708), who claimed that the bison were a wild strain of domestic cattle or, in fact, the already extinct wild ox. With observation and research he set the record straight. Moreover, von Brincken believed that the indigenous bison of Białowieża needed these very surroundings, the herbs and grasses, seeds and barks and undisturbed ecology of the primeval forest in order to survive and breed. Hence the failure of the bison to reproduce when transported abroad.

Despite the exploitation that Białowieża was to suffer in the future, von Brincken's recorded respect of the forest and the life within it undoubtedly helped to protect its very core.

By 1914 the stock of bison had already been depleted to around 460. This was due in part to deforestation and in part to the hunting parties of the tsar. The most damaging of these must have been when the Austrian Archduke Franz Ferdinand decided to "kill two birds with one stone" and test the latest productions from his munitions factory at Styr on the wildlife, machine gunning anything that moved. During the First World War, Białowieża was taken under German "protection." Huge numbers of bison were exported abroad as gifts, for barter or to be exhibited in German zoos. Others were slaughtered as fodder for the starving troops as defeat became imminent. By the end of the war there were just four bison left in the forest. A few years later, in 1921, the last bison of Białowieża died of natural causes.

A century after von Brincken had been busy with his research, a man of similar leaning arrived at Białowieża. Jan Sztolcman was a biologist, fired with a passion for the noble bison and a determination to bring them back to their rightful breeding ground. By 1929, Sztolcman had successfully traced a number of the bison which had been exported to German zoos and organised for their repatriation, together with some bison which had survived in the South of Poland. Independent Poland established the League for Nature Conservation and Białowieża became one of Poland's first three National Parks.

It would be nice if the story ended there but history, as we know, has a habit of repeating itself. Another war and Białowieża found itself back in German hands. Göring took the forest as his personal property, proclaiming it a *Heiliger Hein* — a sacred grove. Now that the animals and birds within it were reclassified as Aryan, strict orders were given that they were not to be touched. The role of the forest had changed. Once a platform for man to test his superiority over beast, it became the scene of appalling warfare between German soldiers, Polish partisans, Soviet partisans and numerous victims from the local population. Mass grave after mass grave was dug among the ancient trees. None better suited as a witness to this genocide than the birch, whose shape Mickiewicz described as:

> *"Like a peasant weeping for her son*
> *Or widow for her husband, as she stands,*
> *Hair streaming to the ground, and wrings her hands*
> *Her silent form than sobs more eloquent"*

In the new shape of post-war Poland, its border with Byelo-Russia ran right through the forest, with the oldest part lying on the Polish side. Security was tight and areas of forest were cleared for guard towers, but Stalin himself had bigger game to hunt than mere bison and elk and after the Moscow State Circus had been unsuccessful in coaxing the bison to perform tricks, they were left in peace. Białowieża is today the last primeval forest in Europe and still a rare haven to herds of elk and bison. Listed by Unesco as a world heritage site, it continues in its defiance against the march of time with Mickiewicz's descriptions of it as apt today as we near the end of the 20th century as they were when written.

"You find a wall of stumps and roots and logs
Defended by a thousand streams and bogs."

Many mournful layers of history have entwined themselves through the forest's floor, but the subjects of the author's cry in *Pan Tadeusz* live on.

"Trees of my fatherland! If heaven will
That I return there, shall I find you still"

It is no wonder, given his love of the forest and the respect with which he treats his ingredients, that Bernard Lussiana should find Białowieża as much of a source of inspiration as others in different walks of life have before him.

The spirit of the forest burns through time and time again in his dishes. Whether it be blackberries from the tangled bushes or hazelnuts from the trees; fruit and petals from the wild rose, earthy mushrooms, forest leaves to wrap the meat in or the aromatic bison grass. Just as these plants, trees and grasses form the stage on which the bison, elk and deer play out their role, on a plate they become the props, each one adding a forest flavour or colour to complement the game they are served with. Their natural habitat preserved, the spirit of the ingredient remains intact.

Unique to Białowieża, bison grass has long been used to flavour Żubrówka vodka. A blade of it bottled with the alcohol is strong enough to infuse the vodka with its herbal overtones of thyme, hyssop and lavender. The grass had never before though been partnered with food. It is every chef's dream to find a new flavour but when Lussiana recognised the opportunity to incorporate this ancient grass, with its characteristic aroma, into his culinary repertoire, it was more than that. It was the perfect building brick for what he was trying to create. A new Polish cuisine with traditional, indigenous ingredients. In October 1995, Lussiana's *Braised rack of suckling pig with Żubrówka grass* won a silver medal at the First Regional Contest of European Flavours held in France, at which 57 other regions competed.

Białowieża had entered culinary history.

Meat and poultry

Fillet of bison roasted in a crust of clay and salt

Braised rack of suckling pig with Żubrówka grass

Ballotine of baby chicken wrapped in beet leaves, served with a chłodnik sauce

Gołąbki of fallow venison, served with a marjoram juice

Bitki of fillet of beef flavoured with grey pepper and Pieprzówka vodka

Escalopes of venison in a crust of hazelnuts, served with a wild rose fruit sauce

Roasted veal shank flavoured with savory and smoked garlic

Goulash of elk "Białowieża style"

Steamed breast of chicken, flavoured with blackcurrant and peppermint

Pan-fried fillet of lamb served with a juice of fresh coriander and saffron kasza

Crunchy purse of guinea fowl and wild mushrooms, served with a spicy juice

Braised kid with horseradish and goats' milk

Fillet of bison roasted in a crust of clay and salt

FILET DE BISON RÔTI EN CROÛTE DE SEL ET GLAISE

A symbol of survival, dwelling in the often impenetrable depths of the primeval forest, bison are now a protected animal rewarded with the respect that their ability to triumph against the odds deserves. In the dish below, the bison's ancient heritage is echoed in the age-old method of cooking meat in a crust of clay and salt, first wrapping it in leaves from its natural habitat to keep the meat moist. Served with mushrooms from the forest floor, it is accompanied by a sauce rich with the aroma of bison grass. Intrinsically forest-like in character, the recipe preserves the spirit of the noble bison — unbroken. The bison used for this recipe are either from those selected for culling from Białowieża or farmed.

2 pounds bison fillet

6 ½ pounds clay

1 pound Wieliczka salt

Salt, pepper

2 ½ tablespoons butter
   to seal the bison

30 maple leaves

For the marinade

⅓ cup sunflower oil

¾ teaspoon juniper berries

½ teaspoon thyme

1 teaspoon hyssop

For the garnish

10 ounces ceps

10 ounces *gąski* (firwood agaric
   mushrooms)

10 ounces parasol mushrooms

2 ½ tablespoons butter

4 teaspoons fresh herbs

For the sauce

⅓ cup white wine

1 teaspoon bison grass

½ teaspoon pink pepper

4 teaspoons dandelion jelly
   (see glossary)

½ cup brown bison stock
   (see glossary)

2 ½ tablespoons butter,
   chilled and diced

For decoration

Maple leaves and bison grass

1   **Three days before:** put the fillet of bison in an earthenware dish. Mix the ingredients together for the marinade
    and pour over the bison. Cover with plastic wrap and leave to marinate for 3 days in refrigerator.

2   **On serving day:** preheat the oven to 550°F. Mix the clay and salt together to form a dough.

3   Clean the three different types of mushrooms and cut them into slices. Pan-fry them in butter with the fresh herbs.

4   Remove the bison from its marinade and pat dry. Season it and seal it in butter in a very hot pan. Remove
    and reserve.

5   Make the sauce: deglaze the pan with the white wine. Add bison grass, pink pepper and the dandelion jelly.
    Leave it to infuse for a few minutes on a very low heat. Add brown stock and season. Finish the sauce
    by whisking in the diced butter, a little at a time until you have a smooth and velvety consistency.

6   Blanch the 30 maple leaves in boiling water. Remove and drain well. Wrap the fillet of bison in the maple leaves.
    Roll out the clay and salt dough and wrap around the bison. Put on a baking tray and cook in the oven
    for 25 minutes.

7   Break open the crust of clay and salt. Carve the bison into slices and arrange on plates with a spoonful of the
    mushrooms. Pour the bison grass sauce around these, decorate with maple leaves and bison grass and serve.

Braised rack of suckling pig with Żubrówka grass

CARRÉ DE COCHON DE LAIT BRAISÉ À L'HERBE DE BISON

Captured in the flavour of this sauce is the characteristic aroma of bison grass. It is an unanswered question as to why the bison grass will only grow in Białowieża, yet all attempts to transplant it elsewhere have failed. Perhaps there is a natural symbiosis between the grass — Herba hierochloe odorata vel australis, as it is known in Latin — in this primeval forest and the existence of the bison. Thriving in patches beneath the canopy of ancient trees, it appears no different from other ordinary grasses and its smell, so immediate when picked and increasingly powerful as it dries, remains hidden whilst it grows. The foresters have ways of recognising it, one of which is when you run your forefinger and thumb up a blade of it, it exudes a milky white liquid. But where to find it is closely guarded information and gathering it is, except by those authorised, forbidden in order to protect this increasingly rare grass from total extinction.

6 chops of suckling pig,
(6 ounces each) trimmed

For the white stock

1 ½ cups onions

1 cup carrots

½ cup celeriac

2 tablespoons bison grass

Bouquet garni (see glossary)

Salt, black peppercorns, cloves

1 tablespoon garlic

For the *paszteciki*

3 pears

3 apples

1 ½ tablespoons butter

1 teaspoon dry pink pepper

1 teaspoon chopped marjoram

1 pound puff pastry

1 large egg, beaten

For the juice

1 ½ teaspoons bison grass

¾ cup white stock from
the suckling pig

½ cup white wine

1 cup brown chicken stock
(see glossary)

1 tablespoon dandelion jelly
(see glossary)

Salt, pepper

2 ½ tablespoons butter

For the garnish

1 pound assorted vegetables
(carrots, leeks, zucchini), sliced
and blanched

For decoration

A few blades of bison grass

1   Prepare the white stock: cut the vegetables into *mirepoix* (see glossary). Add the rest of the stock ingredients
and 5 quarts of water. Bring to the boil and then leave to infuse for 30 minutes. Poach the chops of suckling pig
in the white stock at a temperature of 160°F for 25 minutes.

2   Preheat the oven to 400°F. Prepare the *paszteciki*: peel and chop the pears and apples into *salpicon* (see glossary).
Pan-fry them quickly in the butter with the dry pink pepper and marjoram. Remove from the pan and leave
to cool. Roll out the puff pastry until it is approx. ¼ inch, and make small individual *pithiviers* (see glossary)
with the fruit filling. Brush each one with a little beaten egg and bake in the oven for 12—15 minutes.
Reduce the heat to 300°F.

3   Prepare the juice: infuse the bison grass in the white stock and the white wine. Bring to the boil and reduce
by one-third. Add the brown stock and dandelion jelly and season it. Spoon this juice into a braising pan
with the poached suckling pig and put in the oven for 35 minutes, basting regularly to crisp and glaze the skin.

4   Remove from the oven. Strain the juices into a pan, whisk in a little butter and pour the sauce onto the plates.
Arrange the meat on top and accompany with a small garnish of vegetables, the *paszteciki* and a few blades
of bison grass as decoration.

Ballotine of baby chicken, wrapped in beet leaves, served with a chłodnik sauce

BALLOTINE DE POUSSIN EN HABIT DE FEUILLES DE BETTERAVE ROUGE ET CHŁODNIK

6 baby chickens (approx.
  3/4 pound each)

1 1/2 tablespoons oil

1 cup whole beet leaves

For the chłodnik sauce

5 tablespoons beet leaves,
  cut into fine strips

1/2 cup barszcz, cold
  and prepared with:

1/2 pound beets, cut into slices

1 cup *mirepoix* of celeriac, carrots,
  onions, parsnips (see glossary)

1/3 cup apple, cut into slices

1/2 teaspoon marjoram

2 bay leaves

1 clove garlic, chopped

2 whole cloves

2 tablespoons lemon juice

Pinch of salt, pepper, sugar

3/4 cup heavy cream

3/4 cup natural yoghurt

1 1/2 tablespoons fresh dill, chopped

2 teaspoons fresh chives, chopped

5 tablespoons cucumber, cut into
  julienne (see glossary)

For the stuffing

3/4 cup heavy cream

1/2 teaspoon coriander seeds

7 ounces chicken breasts

2 large egg whites

Salt, pepper

1 pear

1 apple

1 tablespoon lemon juice

3 1/2 ounces chestnuts,
  cooked and coarsely chopped

2 teaspoons honey

1 1/2 teaspoons fresh marjoram,
  chopped

For the garnish

1 pound cooked beets,
  cut into *julienne* (see glossary)

1 Prepare the chłodnik sauce, if possible 24 hours before you need it, so that the flavours have a chance to develop. Blanch the beet leaf strips in boiling water. Remove and reserve them. In the same water cook the remaining sauce ingredients except the cream, yoghurt, dill, chives, and cucumber. Leave to cool and then strain. Stir in the last 5 sauce ingredients. Season to taste and return the blanched beet leaves to the chłodnik. Cover and put in the refrigerator until needed.

2 Preheat the oven to 350°F. Prepare the stuffing: pour half the cream into a small saucepan, add the coriander seeds and over a gentle heat allow to infuse. Strain and leave the cream to cool. Blend the chicken breasts, force them through a fine sieve or muslin and in a bowl set over ice, mix in the egg whites, the remaining cream and the cream infusion. Season and reserve. Peel the pear and apple and chop into cubes of 1/4 inch. Blanch them for 30 seconds in boiling water to which the lemon juice has been added. Drain the fruit and leave to cool. Mix together the chicken mixture, the cubes of fruit, the chestnuts, honey and marjoram. Season to taste and put to one side.

3 Bone the baby chickens, cutting neatly along the breast bone, being careful not to damage their skins. Place each one on a piece of aluminium foil. Season the chicken and fill with the stuffing, pulling the skin over to enclose it. Wrap up in the foil. Heat the oil in a pan and seal the chicken parcels in it. Finish cooking in the oven for 14 minutes. Blanch the whole beet leaves. Remove the chicken from the oven. Remove the foil and cover them with the beet leaves. Cut them into slices. Heat the *julienne* of beets and arrange on plates with a fan of chicken slices and a little chłodnik.

Gołąbki
of fallow venison, served with a marjoram juice

GOŁĄBKI DE DAIM ET JUS À LA MARJOLAINE

"You heard the forest move lazily between pauses of terrifying, bottomless silence. Somewhere a woodpecker was rapping at a tree, a horsefly buzzed; caught in a tangle of flowers, a badger crept past, a fallow deer galloped by, its head held haughtily high, a tree broken by a spring hurricane cracked and fell, a light wind which had strayed into those ancient spaces stirred impatiently."
Tadeusz Konwicki, *The Polish Complex*

1 ³/₄ pounds leg of fallow venison

2 ¹/₂ tablespoons oil

2 ¹/₂ tablespoons flour

1 ¹/₂ tablespoons tomato paste

1 ¹/₂ cups rice

12 leaves savoy cabbage

1 ¹/₃ pounds pekin cabbage

3 tablespoons butter

4 teaspoons fresh marjoram, chopped

1 ¹/₂ cups *mirepoix* of vegetables
(carrots, onions, celeriac;
see glossary)

1 *bouquet garni* (see glossary)

1 teaspoon juniper berries

3 teaspoons marjoram

2 teaspoons garlic

For the marinade

3 ¹/₄ cup red wine

2 tablespoons red wine vinegar

1   Cut the fallow venison into cubes of ³/₄ inch. Mix the ingredients for the marinade together and pour over the venison. Cover with plastic wrap and leave to marinate for 48 hours in refrigerator.

2   With a slotted spoon, remove the venison and vegetables from the marinade. Bring the marinade to the boil, strain it and reserve.

3   Preheat the oven to 300°F. In a very hot pan, pan-fry the venison quickly in the oil. Add the vegetables from the marinade and leave to cook for 5 minutes. Sprinkle the flour over the mixture, stir and cook for a further minute. Add the tomato paste and deglaze with the marinade. Cover the pan and cook for 2 ³/₄ hours in the oven.

4   Cook the rice in boiling water. Strain it and reserve.

5   Blanch the leaves of savoy cabbage in boiling water. Strain them and reserve. Chop the pekin cabbage into cubes and pan-fry them in the butter.

6   When the venison is cooked, strain off ³/₄ cup of sauce and reserve. Chop coarsely the meat and vegetables in the rest of the sauce. Add the rice and the pekin cabbage.

7   Divide this mixture into 6 portions and fill the centre of the savoy cabbage leaves, using two leaves for each portion. Wrap them up carefully into individual parcels. Put in an ovenproof dish with any remaining sauce (apart from that reserved) and bake for 20 minutes.

8   Taste and correct the seasoning of the reserved sauce. Stir in the fresh marjoram. Arrange the gołąbki on plates and spoon the sauce around.

Bitki of fillet of beef flavoured with grey pepper and Pieprzówka vodka

BITKI DE FILET DE BOEUF AU POIVRE GRIS ET VODKA PIEPRZÓWKA

2 pounds fillet of beef

4 teaspoons ground grey pepper

1 ¼ pounds potatoes, peeled

¾ cup heavy cream

¼ teaspoon ground nutmeg

6 tablespoons butter

Salt, pepper

3 tablespoons Pieprzówka vodka

⅓ cup white wine

3 cloves

½ teaspoon fresh marjoram

⅔ cup brown stock (see glossary)

For decoration

Fresh herbs

For the sauce

2 tablespoons sunflower oil

2 tablespoons butter

1 cup *brunoise* of vegetables
   (carrots, onions, celeriac;
   see glossary)

1   Carve the fillet of beef into 18 escalopes. Sprinkle over them the grey pepper.

2   Make the sauce: pour the sunflower oil into a frying pan and when very hot quickly seal the beef escalopes on both
     sides. Remove and reserve. In the same pan, melt the butter and sweat the *brunoise* of vegetables in it. Deglaze
     with the white wine. Add the herbs and brown stock. Slowly reduce the sauce until it has halved in volume.

3   Cook the potatoes in salted, boiling water until tender. Warm the cream in a small saucepan. Drain the potatoes and
     mash them thoroughly, gradually stirring in as you do so the warm cream, nutmeg and finally the butter. Season to taste.

4   Put the beef back into the sauce and flambée it with the vodka. Leave it to cook for 5 minutes.

5   Arrange three escalopes on each plate with the sauce and vegetables. Shape the potato into quenelles
     and add to the plate. Scatter over some fresh herbs as decoration and serve.

Escalopes of venison in a crust of hazelnuts, served with a wild rose fruit sauce

ESCALOPINES DE CHEVREUIL AUX NOISETTES ET CYNORHODONS

*Evocative of a love of autumn and a feeling for the forest, both season and place are reflected
here in the combination of ingredients, colours and texture.
Go to the forest. Smell the fruit of the wild roses in the damp autumn air. Listen in the stillness
for the quick-footed deer. Pull the hazelnuts off the trees. Watch the leaves wave in their melody
of colours and then come home and make this ode to a Polish autumn.*

2 pounds loin of venison, trimmed
   with sinews removed

10 ounces dry brioche

3 ½ ounces whole hazelnuts

1 ⅓ pounds broccoli

2 tablespoons hazelnut oil

2 tablespoons butter

2 tablespoons sliced hazelnuts

For the sauce

½ cup white wine

1 tablespoon red wine vinegar

3 ½ tablespoons rose-hip preserves

⅔ cup game stock (see glossary)

2 bay leaves

Salt, pepper

3 tablespoons butter

For the marinade

2 ½ ounces honey

¾ cup clear vodka (40%)

1 teaspoon juniper berries

1 teaspoon thyme

¾ teaspoon marjoram

4 bay leaves

4 cloves

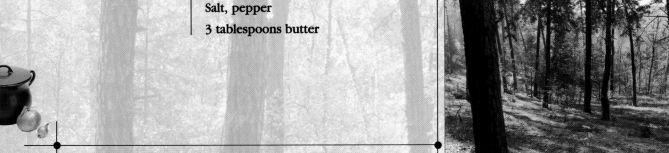

1   Put the loin of venison in an earthenware dish. Make the marinade: warm the honey in the vodka until melted. Add the spices, herbs and when cool, pour over the venison. Cover with plastic wrap and marinate for 48 hours in the refrigerator, turning from time to time.

2   Remove the venison from its marinade and pat dry. Carve the venison into escalopes of ¾ inch thick, (there should be 5 per person) and reserve. In a blender mix the brioche and the whole hazelnuts.

3   Cook the broccoli in a pan of boiling, salted water. Drain well and reserve.

4   In a very hot pan seal the venison escalopes on both sides. Remove and place on a baking tray. Cover each escalope with the hazelnut crust. Dribble over them a little hazelnut oil.

5   Make the sauce: deglaze the pan with the white wine and vinegar. Stir in the rose-hip preserves, game stock and bay leaves. Season to taste and finish the sauce by whisking in 3 tablespoons of butter. Put the venison under a hot grill, for 2—3 minutes.

6   Melt 2 tablespoons butter over a gentle heat in a pan with the sliced hazelnuts. Add the broccoli and toss it with the butter and hazelnuts. Arrange a little broccoli in the middle of each plate with the escalopes of venison in a crescent around it. Pour a touch of sauce onto each plate and serve.

Roasted veal shank flavoured with savory and smoked garlic

JARRET DE VEAU RÔTI À LA SARRIETTE ET AIL FUMÉ

3 pounds veal shank

3 tablespoons oil

3 tablespoons butter

4 tablespoons white wine

2 tablespoons smoked garlic

2 teaspoons savory

Salt, pepper

For the garnish of "knedle"

1 ½ pounds potatoes, with their skins on

1 cup flour

1 large egg

¼ teaspoon nutmeg

Salt, pepper

⅔ cup heavy cream

2 tablespoons black truffles, chopped

For the sauce

5 tablespoons white wine

2 tablespoons smoked garlic

2 ½ teaspoons savory

½ cup brown stock (see glossary)

2 tablespoons butter, chilled and diced

For decoration

Fresh herbs

1   Preheat the oven to 275°F. Seal the veal shank in oil until golden. Add the butter, white wine, smoked garlic and savory and bake for 2 hours. Cover with aluminium foil, and cook for another 30 minutes.

2   Make the garnish: cook the potatoes in a pan of salted boiling water. Drain and peel them. Mash the potatoes, adding flour, egg, nutmeg, salt and pepper as you do so. Shape them into small quenelles and poach them *à la minute* in boiling water. Put the cream and chopped truffles into a pan. Season and reduce by one-third. Five minutes before serving add the potato "knedle" to the cream and let them steep in the flavour.

3   Remove the veal shank from the oven. Remove from the pan and reserve. Make the sauce: pour off the fat from the pan and deglaze with white wine. Add smoked garlic, savory and brown stock. Reduce to a good consistency and whisk in the chilled butter, a little at a time. Carve the veal shank and arrange on individual plates with a touch of sauce and fresh herbs. Serve the potato garnish separately.

Goulash
of elk "Białowieża style"

SAUTÉ D'ÉLAN À LA MODE DE BIAŁOWIEŻA

Elk became extinct across most of Central Europe several centuries ago, but the Białowieża
forest still harbours a number of these magnificent beasts of solitary disposition. Their existence
was threatened under the reign of Tsar Paul I (1796—1801) to whom the forest belonged at the
time, who decided it would be fitting for his Russian Cavalry to be clad in elk-skin breeches.
Luckily the Tsar was to meet his fate before his plan could be executed. Marinated in juniper
berries and thyme, marjoram and pine needles, the elk is served with wild boar bacon and ceps
in a sauce infused with aromatic bison grass and sweetly scented syrup of pine.

2 pounds loin of elk

1 tablespoon bison grass

5 tablespoons white wine

1 ½ tablespoons syrup of pine

²/₃ cup brown game stock
   (see glossary)

1 pound ceps

4 tablespoons butter

Salt, pepper

³/₄ pound brussels sprouts

1 ½ tablespoons sunflower oil

2 ½ ounces small onions

2 ½ ounces wild boar bacon, cubed

2 ½ tablespoons vodka (70%)

For the marinade

½ cup oil

2 teaspoons juniper berries

2 teaspoons pepper

1 teaspoon thyme

1 teaspoon marjoram

1 tablespoon pine needles

For decoration

Chopped fresh herbs

1   Cut the loin of elk into finger-sized strips. Mix all the ingredients for the marinade together. Pour over the elk, cover with plastic wrap, and marinate for 48 hours in the refrigerator.

2   Infuse the bison grass in the white wine and the pine syrup over a very low heat, for 10 minutes to allow the flavours to develop. Add the game stock.

3   Clean and slice the ceps. Pan-fry them in 2 tablespoons of butter and season them.

4   Bring a pan of salted water to the boil and cook the brussels sprouts until just tender. Remove and drain.

5   With a slotted spoon take the strips of elk from its marinade and pat dry. In a very hot pan, quickly pan-fry them in the oil with the onions and bacon. Add the ceps, flambée the mixture with the vodka and deglaze the pan with the sauce. Leave it to cook for 7—10 minutes. Taste and correct seasoning.

6   Over a medium flame, toss the brussels sprouts in 2 tablespoons butter. Arrange a portion of goulash in the middle of each plate. Add the brussels sprouts and decorate with freshly chopped herbs.

Steamed breast of chicken, flavoured with blackcurrant and peppermint

VAPEUR DE BLANC DE VOLAILLE EN SAVEURS DE CASSIS ET MENTHE POIVRÉE

6 chicken breasts (5 ounces each)

4 teaspoons peppermint

$\frac{1}{2}$ cup white chicken stock
(see glossary)

4 tablespoons sugar

$\frac{1}{2}$ cup blackcurrant vinegar

3 tablespoons blackcurrants

6 tablespoons brown stock
(see glossary)

For the stuffing

5 ounces chicken breast

1 large egg white

$\frac{2}{3}$ cup heavy cream

Salt, pepper

2 teaspoons fresh mint, chopped

6 courgette flowers

For decoration

Blackcurrant and mint leaves

Here's flowers for you;
Hot lavender, mints, savory, marjoram;
The marigold that goes to bed wi' the sun
And with him rises weeping.

William Shakespeare, *The Winter's Tale*

1   Make the stuffing for the courgette flowers: blend the 5 ounces of chicken breast and force through a fine sieve or muslin. In a bowl, set over ice, mix in the egg white and cream. Season the mixture and add the chopped mint.

2   Remove the blossom from the inside of the flowers and using a piping bag, fill the flowers with the chicken mixture. Put to one side.

3   Make a small slit in the side of each chicken breast, so as to create a pocket inside them. Fill this with the peppermint. Season them and put each breast on a square of plastic wrap. Baste them with two spoons of chicken stock and fold the plastic wrap over them securely. Reserve.

4   Melt the sugar in a heavy bottomed pan. Deglaze with the blackcurrant vinegar. Allow the caramel to dissolve and add 1 $\frac{1}{2}$ tablespoons of the blackcurrants and the brown stock. Infuse for 15 minutes.

5   In a steamer, or on a rack over boiling water, covered, steam the courgette flowers for 6 minutes and the chicken breasts for 9 minutes.

6   Cut the courgette flowers in half and cut the chicken breasts into slices. Arrange on the plates.

7   Strain the sauce and pour a little on each plate, adding the remaining, 1 $\frac{1}{2}$ tablespoons blackcurrants. Decorate with blackcurrant and mint leaves and serve.

Pan-fried
fillet of lamb served with a juice of fresh coriander and saffron kasza

FILET D'AGNEAU EN SAVEURS DE CORIANDRE FRAIS ET KASHA SAFRANNÉ

*Stanisław August, famous for his contribution to the arts, was also renowned as a gourmet.
His chef, Pawel Tremo, considered in the Warsaw of the time as the finest chef in Europe combined
traditional Polish food with French influences and techniques to please the palate of the Francophile
king. Lamb was the king's favourite meat and variations of it were frequently served by Tremo at
the "Thursday Dinner" gatherings of intellectuals at the Royal Castle and Łazienki Palace.*

6 racks of lamb with bones
(1/2 pound each)

3 tablespoons clarified butter
(see glossary)

3 1/2 ounces dry white bread

2 tablespoons, fresh parsley

2 teaspoons fresh coriander

1 1/2 tablespoons mustard

For the marinade

4 tablespoons olive oil

1 sprig rosemary

1 sprig thyme

1 sprig marjoram

1 clove garlic

For the garnish

4 tablespoons butter

10 ounces white *kasza*

4 tablespoons white wine

1 1/4 cups white chicken stock
(see glossary)

3/4 cup heavy cream

1/2 teaspoon saffron

Salt, pepper

For the sauce

4 tablespoons white wine

2 teaspoons fresh coriander

1/2 cup brown lamb stock
(see glossary)

2 tablespoons butter, chilled
and diced

For decoration

Fresh coriander leaves

1 Place the lamb in an earthenware dish. Mix the ingredients for the marinade and pour over the lamb. Cover with plastic wrap and refrigerate for 36 hours.

2 Preheat the oven to 350°F. Prepare the garnish: melt the butter in a heavy bottomed saucepan. Add the *kasza* and cook for a minute before deglazing with the white wine. Add the chicken stock, cream, saffron and seasoning and cook slowly over a gentle heat until ready.

3 Remove the lamb from the marinade, reserving the herbs, and pat dry. Seal the lamb in a hot pan with the clarified butter and then place in a roasting tray with the herbs from the marinade and cook in the oven for 13 minutes. When cooked, remove the lamb and reserve (but leave the oven on).

4 Prepare the sauce: skim off the fat from the roasting tray and deglaze it with the white wine. Add the fresh coriander and lamb stock and allow to infuse slowly.

5 Crumble the dried bread into breadcrumbs and blend with the parsley and coriander. Coat the lamb with a little mustard and cover this with the breadcrumb mixture. Put the lamb back into a hot oven for 5 minutes to seal the crust.

6 Strain the sauce and check the seasoning. Whisk in the chilled butter. Carve the lamb into slices and arrange on the plates with a mound of saffron *kasza* and a touch of sauce around. Decorate with some fresh coriander leaves and serve.

Crunchy purse
of guinea fowl and wild mushrooms, served with a spicy juice

CROUSTILLANT DE PINTADEAU ET TRICHOLOMES DORÉS, UN JUS EPICÉ

2 ½ pounds guinea fowl

1 cup *mirepoix* of vegetables (carrots, celeriac, onions; see glossary)

1 tablespoon tomato paste

½ cup red wine

1 *bouquet garni* (see glossary)

9 ounces strudel dough (see glossary)

3 ½ tablespoons clarified butter (see glossary)

For the stuffing

4 ½ ounces chicken breast

½ cup heavy cream

1 large egg white

2 tablespoons plus 2 teaspoons fresh herbs

Salt, pepper

10 ounces *gąski* (firwood agaric mushrooms)

For the garnish

1 ¼ pounds *gąski*

4 teaspoons fresh herbs

3 tablespoons butter

For the sauce

6 tablespoons white wine

¼ teaspoon each of turmeric, curry, cardamom, paprika, chili powder

1 ½ tablespoons honey

½ cup brown stock

2 teaspoons white wine vinegar

3 tablespoons butter, chilled and diced

For decoration

Pinch of spices: turmeric, curry, cardamom, paprika, chili powder

Fresh herbs, chopped

---

1   Preheat the oven to 300°F. Bone the guinea-fowl taking care not to damage the skin. Reserve the meat. Make a brown stock with the bones by roasting them on a roasting tray in the oven until golden. Add the *mirepoix* of vegetables and the tomato paste. Reduce the heat to 275°F and cook for another hour.

2   Deglaze the bones in the roasting tray with the red wine. Put in a saucepan with 1 quart of cold water and the *bouquet garni*. Cook for 1 hour. Strain and reduce the stock to ½ cup and reserve for step 5.

3   Raise the oven to 300°F. Prepare the stuffing: blend the chicken breast and force it through a fine sieve. In a bowl over ice, mix in the cream and egg white. Add 2 teaspoons of chopped herbs and season. Clean and slice the mushrooms. Pan-fry them with 2 tablespoons chopped herbs and cool before mixing in to the chicken.

4   Spread the boned guinea fowl out on a sheet of greased aluminium foil. Spoon the stuffing onto the meat and roll it up to 2 ½ inches. Wrap the guinea fowl up in the foil and tie string around it at ¾ inch intervals. Cook in the oven for 22 minutes. Remove the guinea fowl from the oven. Remove foil. Roll out the strudel dough and encase the guinea fowl roulade in it. Deep-fry this in clarified butter.

5   Prepare the sauce: pour the white wine into a small saucepan. Add spices and honey and leave to infuse for a few minutes. Add the reserved brown stock and cook slowly over a low heat. Check seasoning. Add the vinegar and whisk in butter to a smooth consistency.

6   Cut the purse of guinea fowl into slices and arrange on plates with a spoon of mushrooms and a touch of sauce. Dust the edges of the plates with spices. Sprinkle on fresh herbs and serve.

Braised kid with horseradish and goats' milk

CABRI BRAISÉ AU RAIFORT ET LAIT DE CHÈVRE

½ goat kid (approx. 6 ½ pounds)

4 tablespoons sunflower oil

For the sauce

2 ½ tablespoons onions, chopped

2 ½ tablespoons butter

4 tablespoons horseradish puree

2 teaspoons sugar

1 tablespoon mustard

2 teaspoons garlic

1 *bouquet garni* (see glossary)

½ cup white wine

1 ¼ cups goats' milk

½ cup heavy cream

Salt, pepper

2 tablespoons clear vodka (40%)

For the garnish

1 ¾ pounds Jerusalem artichokes

2 tablespoons lemon juice

2 ½ tablespoons butter

4 teaspoons fresh herbs, chopped

For decoration

Fresh herbs

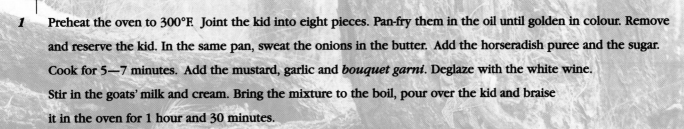

1   Preheat the oven to 300°F. Joint the kid into eight pieces. Pan-fry them in the oil until golden in colour. Remove
and reserve the kid. In the same pan, sweat the onions in the butter. Add the horseradish puree and the sugar.
Cook for 5—7 minutes. Add the mustard, garlic and *bouquet garni*. Deglaze with the white wine.
Stir in the goats' milk and cream. Bring the mixture to the boil, pour over the kid and braise
it in the oven for 1 hour and 30 minutes.

2   Prepare the garnish: peel the Jerusalem artichokes and cook them in boiling water with the lemon juice until tender.
Remove, drain and reserve. Melt the butter and toss the Jerusalem artichokes in it with the chopped fresh herbs.

3   Carve the kid into portions giving every person a piece of rack, leg and shoulder.

4   Strain the sauce. Check the seasoning. Stir in the vodka. Arrange the Jerusalem artichokes on the plates
with the portions of kid alongside them. Pour a little sauce around them and decorate with some fresh herbs.

Desserts

Dream around a rose

•

Honey delights

•

Layers of dark chocolate mousse and lavender ice cream

•

Shortbread lily biscuits with yoghurt sorbet

•

Warm gingerbread souffle, served with a blood orange coulis

•

Fantasy around a beet

•

Rhubarb and wild strawberry sabayon, served with its own sorbet

•

Duet

•

Opera of Warsaw

•

Harlequin of three vodkas

•

Iced parfait flavoured with zbożowa coffee

•

Mille-feuille of white chocolate mousse with pink peppercorns and Pieprzówka vodka

---

Dream around a rose

RÊVERIE AUTOUR D'UNE ROSE

Serves 8

For the rose pulp

18 ounces rose petals
1 ¼ cups sugar
3 ½ tablespoons water

For the rose sorbet

⅔ cup sugar
2 cups water
6 ½ ounces rose petals

For the rose jam

18 ounces sugar
2 tablespoons pectin
1 cup water
1 ⅓ pounds rose pulp *(see above)*
2 tablespoons lemon juice

For the rose jelly

¾ cup water
3 ½ tablespoons sugar
½ ounce gelatine leaves,
   softened in cold water
⅓ cup rose water
3 teaspoons *julienne*
   of rose petals

For the pistachio biscuit

4 large egg yolks
2 tablespoons pistachio paste*
5 ounces ground almonds
1 tablespoon flour
1 tablespoon butter, melted
4 large egg whites
⅔ cup sugar

For the rose mousse

⅔ cup sugar
4 tablespoons water
3 large egg whites
1 ½ ounces gelatine leaves,
   softened in cold water
1 ¼ cups whipped cream
1 ¼ cups strained rose jam
   (see above)

For the sweet pastry

5 tablespoons butter
1 cup confectioners sugar
2 teaspoons potato flour
1 large egg
1 ½ cups white flour
2 teaspoons milk

For decoration

1 cup rose petal vodka
Rose petals

1   **Three days before:** prepare the rose pulp. Blend the rose petals with sugar and water. Bring to the boil, remove from the heat and pour into a suitable container. Allow to steep for three days in the refrigerator.

2   **Two days before:** prepare the base for the rose sorbet. Bring the sugar and water to the boil. Remove from the heat. Add the rose petals, cover and let it infuse for 20 minutes. Blend it, leave to cool and reserve in the refrigerator for two days.

3   **On serving day:** strain the rose sorbet through a fine sieve and churn in a sorbetiere or put to freeze in a freezer, beating well once when it is semi-frozen.

4   Preheat the oven to 300°F.

5   Make the rose jam: remove the rose pulp from the refrigerator. Mix the sugar with the pectin, add water and the rose pulp. Bring to the boil and continue to boil rapidly until the temperature reaches 226°F. Add the lemon juice and stir. Divide the mixture into two. Strain one and reserve both.

6   Prepare the rose jelly: bring the water to the boil, add the sugar and let it dissolve. Take it off the heat add the softened gelatine and rose water and leave to cool until it is room temperature. At that point and when it is beginning to set, stir in the julienne of roses. Pour into individual ramekin dishes and reserve in the refrigerator.

7   Prepare the pistachio biscuit: beat the egg yolks with the pistachio paste and ground almonds. Add flour and the melted butter. Whisk the egg whites until they hold stiff peaks, whisking in the sugar at the end. Carefully fold in the egg whites to the egg yolk mixture and spoon onto greaseproof paper. Put in the preheated oven for 12—15 minutes. Take out and leave to cool.

8   Prepare the rose mousse: dissolve the sugar in the water and boil until it reaches 250°F. Meanwhile, whisk the egg whites and when the caramel is ready, pour onto the egg whites continuing to whisk. Add the softened gelatine and carry on whisking until the mixture has reached room temperature. Carefully fold in the whipped cream and the strained rose jam.

9   Into the bottom of eight 2 ½ inch round forms put a layer of pistachio biscuit and top with the rose mousse, smoothing to make it even. Reserve in the refrigerator.

10 Prepare the sweet pastry: mix the butter thoroughly with the sugar, potato flour and egg. Add flour and milk. Knead it well and leave to rest for two hours.

11 Preheat the oven to 325°F.

12 On a lightly floured board, roll out the dough to a thickness of ⅛ inch. Fill eight tartlet moulds with the dough and bake for 7—9 minutes. Remove and reserve. When cool, fill with the unstrained rose jam.

13 On each plate arrange one mousse of roses, one jelly of roses, a tartlet filled with rose jam, a scoop of rose sorbet and a small liqueur glass filled with rose petal vodka. Decorate with rose petals.

This can be made at home by mixing shelled and skinned pistachio nuts with sufficient drops of oil, in the blender, to achieve a paste.

The rose petal vodka in this dish comes from the £ancut distillery, founded in 1784, which was famed for this production from before the Second World War. Flavoured with attar of roses, which pound for pound is worth more than its weight in gold, it is a sensual, smoothly per-fumed liqueur. With a basket brimful of rose petals, the variety of different culinary combina-tions that can be created is shown in this Dream around a rose.

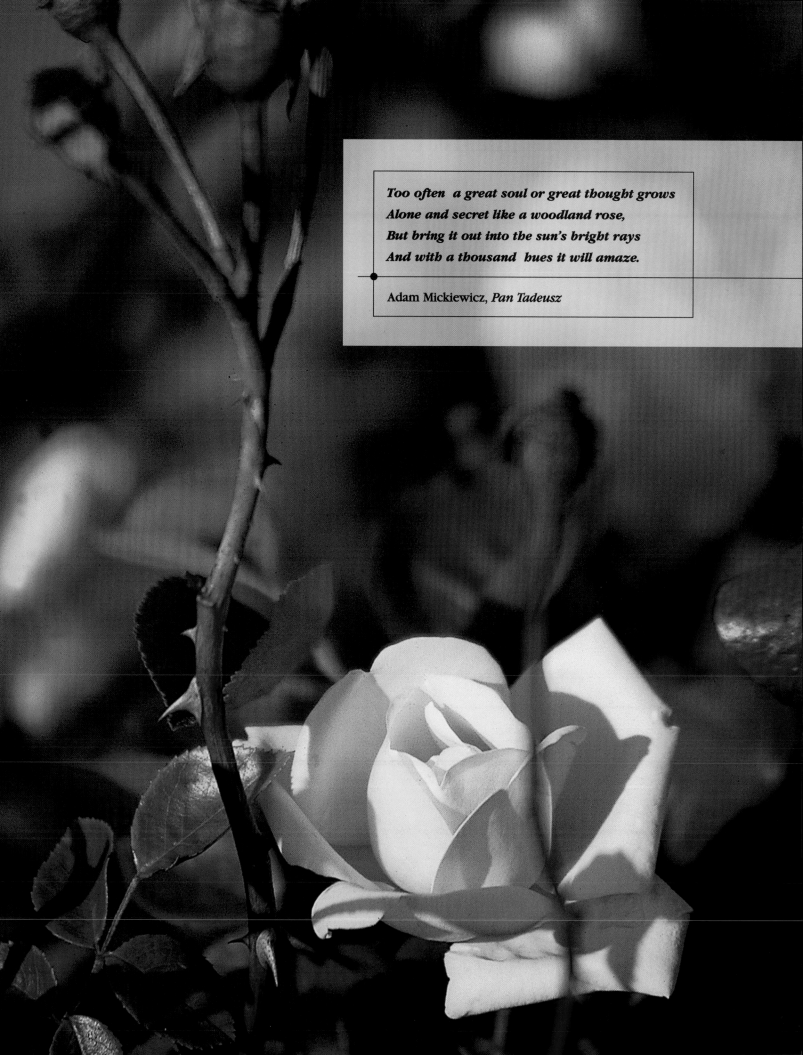

Too often a great soul or great thought grows
Alone and secret like a woodland rose,
But bring it out into the sun's bright rays
And with a thousand hues it will amaze.

Adam Mickiewicz, *Pan Tadeusz*

Honey delights

DÉLICE AUX MIELS

Serves 8

1 pound puff pastry

1 large egg yolk, beaten

½ pound acacia honey

For the mousse of buckwheat honey

10 ounces buckwheat honey

4 tablespoons water

6 large egg whites

1 ounce of gelatine,
   softened in cold water

2 tablespoons orange juice

2 tablespoons lemon juice

2 cups whipped heavy cream

For the honey ice cream

5 large egg yolks

6 ½ ounces lime blossom honey

2 cups milk

1 cup light cream

For decoration

Flowers of the different honeys,
according to the season

1   Prepare the mousse: heat the buckwheat honey with the water until it reaches a temperature of 250°F. Whisk the egg whites until they form stiff peaks and slowly pour on the melted honey, whisking all the time. While the mixture is still hot enough to dissolve the gelatine, stir it in and then leave to cool. Add orange and lemon juice.

2   When it is almost cold, carefully fold in the whipped cream and pour it into a triangular mould, lined with plastic wrap.

3   Make the ice cream: beat the egg yolks with the honey. Heat the milk to boiling point and pour onto the yolks. Cook over a gentle flame until the mixture coats the back of a metal spoon. Leave to cool. Churn it in an ice cream maker or mix thoroughly and put into the freezer. When the ice cream has started to set, mix in the cream thoroughly and either return to the freezer until set or finish in the ice cream maker.

4   Preheat the oven to 425°F.

5   Roll out the puff pastry to a thickness of ¼ inch. Cut it into a lattice pattern. Brush with the egg yolk and put on greaseproof paper in the oven for 8—11 minutes.

6   Cut the mousse into 8 small pyramids and arrange on the plates. Cut out 8 leaves from the puff pastry. Against each pyramid stand a leaf of puff pastry and baste the top with the liquid honey. Add two spoons of ice cream to the plates.

7   Decorate with a scattering of flowers and serve.

Layers of dark chocolate mousse and lavender ice cream

FEUILLANTINE AU CHOCOLAT AMER ET LAIT GLACÉ À LA LAVANDE

Serves 8

For the chocolate mousse

8 ³/₄ ounces dark chocolate,
   extra bitter
3 large egg yolks, beaten
4 large egg whites
5 teaspoons sugar
³/₄ cup whipped heavy cream

For the lavender ice cream

¹/₂ cup whole milk
1 teaspoon lavender
³/₄ cup heavy cream
¹/₂ cup, unsweetened
   condensed milk
5 teaspoons sugar

For the physalis *coulis*

4 ¹/₂ ounces gooseberries
10 ounces physalis
   (cape gooseberries)
4 teaspoons sugar

For the chocolate layers

8 ounces dark chocolate
   (*couverture*)

For the decoration

3 tablespoons lavender
   sprigs
1 large egg white, beaten
4 tablespoons sugar
A few physalis

1 Make the chocolate mousse: break up the chocolate and melt in a *bain-marie* (see glossary).
   Take off the heat and mix in the egg yolks. Whisk the egg whites until stiff, adding the sugar at the end.
   Fold in the chocolate carefully and when well blended and smooth, add the whipped cream. Reserve.

2 Make the lavender ice cream: pour the milk into a saucepan, add the lavender and infuse on a low heat.
   Strain, whisk in the cream, condensed milk and sugar. Churn in an ice cream maker. Freeze.

3 Make the physalis *coulis*: in a saucepan crush the gooseberries and physalis with the sugar.
   Bring to the boil. Blend, strain and leave to cool.

4 Make the chocolate layers: melt the chocolate in a *bain-marie*. Cover a tray with plastic wrap and pour
   on a ¹/₈ inch layer of chocolate. Leave to cool. Cut out 32 circles of chocolate of 2 ³/₄ inches each.

5 Make the decoration: brush the sprigs of lavender with the beaten egg white.
   Sprinkle them with the sugar and put in warm place to dry.

6 Assemble the layers. Begin with a chocolate circle, then a layer of chocolate mousse, top this with another
   chocolate circle and put on a layer of lavender ice cream. Cover that with another chocolate circle and top
   it with a layer of chocolate mousse. Finish with a chocolate circle. Arrange on plates. Pour a little *coulis* around
   each and decorate with the candied lavender and a few physalis. Serve the rest of the ice cream separately.

Shortbread lily biscuits with yoghurt sorbet

SABLÉS À LA FLEUR DE LILIA ET SORBET AU YOGOURT

For the shortbread pastry

3 large egg yolks, hard-boiled
2 teaspoons lily blossoms, chopped
4 tablespoons sugar
4 1/4 ounces butter, softened
4 1/2 ounces flour
Lily water

For the yoghurt sorbet

3/4 cup whole milk
5 tablespoons sugar
3/4 cup whole milk natural
   yoghurt

For decoration

Lilies
1 large egg white, beaten
Sugar

You prefer innocence –
There are lilies.

Maria Pawlikowska-Jasnorzewska, *Świat mówi*

1   Prepare the shortbread pastry: mash the egg yolks and mix with the chopped lily blossoms and sugar. Mix in the softened butter until well blended. Slowly sift in the flour, incorporating it with your fingertips, until you have a crumbly, sandy dough. Add just enough lily water to bind the dough. Knead on a lightly floured surface and shape the dough into a ball. Wrap in plastic wrap and chill in the refrigerator for 3 hours.

2   Meanwhile make the sorbet: bring the milk to the boil, add the sugar and let it dissolve. Remove from the heat and let it cool before mixing in the yoghurt. Churn in a sorbetiere or mix thoroughly and freeze, mixing well once again when semi-frozen.

3   Finish the biscuits: roll out the dough to a thickness of 1/4 inch. Carefully cut out twelve "butterfly wings," using a cardboard form if easier. Cover a baking tray with greaseproof paper and lay the wings on it. Leave to stand for 2 hours at room temperature.

4   Preheat the oven to 300°F. Put the biscuits into the oven and cook for 13—18 minutes. Leave to cool.

5   For the decoration: brush the petals of the lilies with the beaten egg white and sprinkle with sugar. Reserve.

6   Shape the sorbet into quenelles, like the body of a butterfly, and put one in the centre of each plate. On either side of the sorbet arrange a butterfly wing and decorate with the candied lilies.

Warm gingerbread souffle, served with a blood orange coulis

SOUFFLÉ CHAUD AU PAIN D´ÉPICES ET COULIS GLACÉ D'ORANGES SANGUINES

*Gingerbread has always had an aura of mystery and magic, which makes it a particularly
appropriate ingredient for a souffle with its own seemingly mystical properties.
Ever since ginger was discovered it has been featured as much in literature as on the table.
It is described as an aphrodisiac in the stories of the Arabian Nights
and was mentioned by Marco Polo who wrote of honeyed
and candied ginger found on his travels in China.*

For the crème pâtissière

$^1/_2$ cup whole milk

$^1/_2$ cup heavy cream

$^1/_4$ teaspoon gingerbread spices

3 large egg yolks

4 teaspoons sugar

4 teaspoons flour

For the gingerbread

2 tablespoons milk

4 tablespoons honey

2 teaspoons gingerbread spices

4 large egg yolks

3 tablespoons sugar

$^2/_3$ cup flour

2 teaspoons baking powder

2 teaspoons orange zest,
  chopped finely

For the blood orange coulis

2 cups blood orange juice

$^3/_4$ cup sugar

For the souffle

8 $^1/_2$ ounces *crème pâtissière*
(see above)

2 tablespoons gingerbread,
(see above) grated

10 large egg whites

2 tablespoons sugar, plus additional
  for sprinkling

1   Make the *crème pâtissière*: bring the milk, cream and spices to the boil. Whisk the yolks and sugar
together until pale and then whisk in the flour. Pour the boiling milk and cream onto the yolk mixture
and whisk until well blended, Bring back to the boil and cook for 6—7 minutes. Leave to cool.

2   Preheat the oven to 300°F. Prepare the gingerbread: in a small saucepan bring the milk, honey and spices to the
boil. Whisk the egg yolks and sugar together and add. Whisk in the flour, baking powder and orange zest. Mix
well and pour into a loaf tin lined with greaseproof paper. Put in the oven for 30—35 minutes.
Remove and leave to cool, but turn up the oven to 400°F, to preheat for the souffle.

3   Make the blood orange *coulis*: put the blood orange juice and sugar into a saucepan. Heat until the sugar
dissolves. Bring to the boil and simmer until reduced to 1 $^1/_4$ cups. Remove from the heat and allow to cool.

4   Mix together the *crème pâtissière* with the grated gingerbread. Whisk the egg whites until stiff with the sugar.
Grease six individual souffle dishes (of 8 ounces capacity) with butter and sprinkle the insides with sugar. Pour
in the souffle mixture and bake for 20 minutes. Serve immediately and hand the *coulis* round separately.

Fantasy around a beet

FANTAISIE AUTOUR D'UNE BETTERAVE ROUGE

Serves 8

6 cups red wine

1 ½ cups sugar

7 cloves

2 teaspoons fresh thyme

1 teaspoon cardamom, whole

1 teaspoon whole cinnamon stick

8 beets (approx. 7 ounces each)

For the elderflower syrup

2 ½ cups water

1 ½ cups sugar

1 tablespoon lemon juice

6 ½ ounces elderflowers

¾ ounce gelatine,
  softened in cold water

For the saffron *crème brûlée*

3 cups heavy cream

1 teaspoon saffron threads

9 large egg yolks

6 tablespoons granulated sugar

1 tablespoon brown sugar

For decoration

Mint leaves and a scattering
  of gold leaf

1   Make a syrup with the red wine, sugar, herbs and spices. Peel the beets, cut off the tops, reserving them, and hollow out the insides. Poach the beets with their tops in the prepared syrup until tender. Take the pan off the heat and allow the beets to cool while still in the syrup.

2   Make the elderflower syrup: Bring the water to the boil, with the sugar and lemon juice added. Chop the elderflowers coarsely and add them. Take off the heat, cover the saucepan and leave the syrup to infuse for 20 minutes. Strain it, add the gelatine and when it dissolves, leave the mixture to cool.

3   Make the *crème brûlée*: Put the cream and saffron threads into a saucepan and bring to the boil. Whisk the egg yolks with the granulated sugar. Pour on the cream and mix thoroughly. Return to the heat and cook gently until the mixture has reached a coating consistency. Leave to cool.

4   Drain the beets. Fill them with the saffron *crème brûlée*. Sprinkle the brown sugar on top and put under a very hot grill to caramelise the tops. Replace the beet tops.

5   Pour a little elderflower syrup onto each plate and stand the beets in the middle. Decorate and serve.

Rhubarb and wild strawberry sabayon, served with its own sorbet

SABAYON DE RHUBARBE ET FRAISES DES BOIS, UN SORBET DE SAISON

Wild strawberries were once the only strawberry but demand was greater than supply and so the modern strawberry was born. Introduced to Europe in 1821 it was a hybrid between the tasty wild scarlet strawberry found in Virgina and large fruiting, blander strawberry from Chile. Wild strawberries remain a gift from the gods, untouched by human hands except for that heavenly task of collecting them, fragrant and juicy, fresh from the forest floor. In Poland, they still grow in such abundance that in summer the soft forest air is permeated by their sweet scent.

126

10 ounces rhubarb

$^1/_2$ cup water

$^2/_3$ cup sugar

10 ounces wild strawberries

$^1/_2$ cup whipped cream

• For the sorbet

1 pound wild strawberries

$^1/_2$ cup water

1 cup sugar

2 tablespoons lemon juice

• For the *sabayon*

5 large egg yolks

2 tablespoons sugar

$^1/_3$ cup white wine (muscat)

The great hearts of the rhubarb quake.

Maria Pawlikowska-Jasnorzewska, *Pyszne lato*

1   Prepare the sorbet: steep the pound of wild strawberries in the water, sugar and lemon juice for half a day. Blend in a mixer and either churn in a sorbietiere or put in the freezer until semi-frozen, then beat again and return to the freezer.

2   Peel the rhubarb and cut the stalks into segments of 1 inch. Bring the water and $^2/_3$ cup sugar to the boil, turn down to simmering point and poach the rhubarb in this for 3—5 minutes. Drain the rhubarb and reserve.

3   Make the *sabayon*: place the egg yolks, sugar and white wine in a *bain-marie* (see glossary) and whisk at a very high speed until a temperature of 143°F is reached or it has tripled in volume.

4   Place a ring of rhubarb around the edge of 6 soup plates. Arrange the wild strawberries in the middle. Gently fold the whipped cream into the *sabayon* and cover the rhubarb and strawberries with it.

5   Glaze under a very hot grill for 30 seconds and serve. Serve the sorbet separately.

Duet

"DUET" MOUSSE DE FROMAGE BLANC ET GRAINES DE PAVOT BLEU

Serves 8

For the poppy seed base

5 ¹/₂ ounces poppy seeds

1 cup milk

2 large eggs

1 tablespoon butter

3 tablespoons honey

1 ¹/₂ tablespoons sugar

1 tablespoon raisins

5 drops vanilla extract

2 drops almond extract

For the cream cheese mousse

4 ounces sugar

4 tablespoons water

6 large egg yolks, beaten

1 ounce gelatine,
    softened in cold water

6 ounces cream cheese

²/₃ cup yoghurt

1 ¹/₂ cups whipped heavy cream

For the grapefruit sauce

³/₄ cup grapefruit juice

4 tablespoons water

4 tablespoons sugar

¹/₂ ounce gelatine,
    softened in cold water

1 Preheat the oven to 300°F. Prepare the poppy seed base: simmer the poppy seeds in the milk until
the milk has completely evaporated. Blend the mixture three times until you have a fine paste. Stir in the eggs,
butter, honey, sugar, raisins. Add the vanilla and almond extracts. Mix together thoroughly and spoon into
an 11 inch round form on greaseproof paper. Put in the oven to cook for 12—15 minutes.

2 Make the cream cheese mousse: put the sugar and water into a saucepan and stir over a medium heat until it has
reached a temperature of 250°F. Pour it slowly onto the beaten egg yolks, whisking fast all the time as you do so.
Add the gelatine and continue to whisk until the mixture has reached room temperature. Whisk the cream
cheese and yoghurt together and mix into the egg yolks. Add the whipped cream. Pour onto the top
of the poppy seed base and smooth out the surface evenly. Reserve in the refrigerator.

3 Make the sauce: bring the grapefruit juice and water to the boil. Add the sugar and gelatine and let
them dissolve stirring from time to time. Leave to cool.

4 With a form, cut out varying sizes of the Duet so that you can arrange a gradation on the plates. Spoon a little
of the grapefruit sauce onto each plate. Arrange the Duet on top and brush it with a little bit of the sauce.

Opera of Warsaw

OPÉRA DE VARSOVIE

Serves 8

For the madeleine biscuit

8 large egg yolks

5 tablespoons sugar

3 1/2 ounces honey

6 tablespoons butter, softened

1/2 cup plus 1 tablespoon flour

1 1/2 teaspoons baking powder

3 drops vanilla extract

For the poppy seed extract

1 pound poppy seeds

6 cups (1 1/2 quarts) milk

For the poppy seed mousse

2/5 cup water

2 1/2 cups sugar

7 large egg whites

1 1/2 ounces gelatine leaves, softened
   in cold water

1 cup poppy seed extract *(see above)*

1 1/2 cups whipped heavy cream

4 tablespoons Pieprzówka vodka

For the violet sorbet

2 cups water

3/4 cup sugar

3 1/2 ounces candied violets

For the chocolate case

7 ounces dark chocolate

1 3/4 ounces white chocolate

For decoration

3 ounces chocolate for the lines of music

2 ounces candied violets

Mint leaves

1 Preheat the oven to 300°F. Make the madeleine biscuit: whisk together thoroughly the egg yolks, sugar and honey. Mix in the softened butter, flour, baking powder and vanilla extract and pour a 1/2 inch layer onto a baking tray lined with greaseproof paper. Leave for 30 minutes then put in the oven for 15—20 minutes. Remove from the oven and leave to cool.

2 Prepare the poppy seed extract: boil the poppy seeds and milk together, strain and leave to cool.

3 For the mousse: bring the water and sugar to the boil and cook to 250°F. Whisk the egg whites until stiff and pour the caramel gently onto the egg whites, whisking all the time. Whisk in the gelatine until it dissolves. Carefully fold in the poppy seed extract, whipped cream and vodka. Cut the biscuit into two equal halves. Put the poppy seed mousse on top of one and cover it with the second half of biscuit. Reserve in the refrigerator.

4 Make the violet sorbet: bring the water and sugar to the boil. Take off the heat and add the candied violets; let them melt. Strain, leave to cool and then churn in a sorbetiere. Reserve in the freezer.

5 Melt the chocolates separately. On plastic wrap spread the white chocolate and cover this with a thin layer of dark chocolate. When cool cut out 8 violin shapes. Cut out another 8 violin shapes from the madeleine biscuit and cover these with the chocolate forms. Onto each plate, pipe a few lines of music with dark chocolate. Arrange the violin on the plates with several small balls of sorbet. Decorate with candied violets and mint leaves.

Harlequin of three vodkas

ARLEQUIN AUX TROIS VODKAS

*"He left a bottle on the tray. I looked at it, and it was that Polish stuff
you'd all talked about at the Ritz.*

Żubrówka

*You'd all raved how good it smelt and I was curious. I took out the cork and had a sniff.
You were quite right; it smelt damned good...Then I thought I'd just pour out a glass
and look at it. It had such a pretty colour...its colour is just like its smell.
It's like the green you sometimes see in the heart of a white rose."*

W. Somerset Maugham, *The Razor's Edge*

Serves 12

For the Pieprzówka layer

2/3 cup sugar

5 tablespoons water

4 large egg whites

2/3 cup sugar

5 tablespoons water

4 large egg yolks

1/2 cup Pieprzówka vodka

1/4 teaspoon ground grey pepper

1 cup whipped heavy cream

For the Żubrówka layer

2/3 cup sugar

5 tablespoons water

4 large egg whites

2/3 cup sugar

5 tablespoons water

4 large egg yolks

1/2 cup Żubrówka vodka

1/2 teaspoon bison grass, chopped

1 cup whipped heavy cream

For the Czarna Porzeczka layer

2/3 cup sugar

5 tablespoons water

4 large egg whites

2/3 cup sugar

5 tablespoons water

4 large egg yolks

1/2 cup blackcurrant vodka

2 ounces blackcurrants

1 cup whipped heavy cream

1   Make the Pieprzówka layer. First step: heat the sugar with the water to 250°F. Whisk the egg whites until stiff and pour the sugar mixture onto them. Continue to whisk until the mixture has reached room temperature. Second step: heat the sugar with the water to 250°F. Beat the egg yolks and pour the sugar mixture onto them. Continue to whisk until the mixture has reached room temperature.

2   Third step: Mix the two mixtures from above together. Add the Pieprzówka vodka, the pepper and carefully fold in the whipped cream. Reserve.

3   Make the Żubrówka layer: repeat the first, second and third steps as above. Add the Żubrówka vodka, chopped bison grass and carefully fold in the whipped cream. Reserve.

4   Make the Czarna Porzeczka layer: repeat the first, second and thirds steps as above. Add the blackcurrant vodka and the blackcurrants. Carefully fold in the whipped cream.

5   Pour alternate layers of the harlequin into a triangular mould and freeze.

6   Slice harlequin into 12 portions and serve immediately.

Iced parfait flavoured with zbożowa coffee

PARFAIT GLACÉ AU CAFÉ ZBOŻOWA

Serves 12

To make the zbożowa extract

$^1/_2$ pound zbożowa coffee

2 cups water

For the *succes* biscuit

4 egg whites

$^1/_2$ cup sugar

6 tablespoons ground hazelnuts

For the iced parfait

$^1/_2$ cup water

2 cups sugar

16 large egg whites

16 large egg yolks

3 $^1/_4$ cups whipped heavy cream

$^2/_3$ cup zbożowa extract *(see above)*

For the zbożowa sauce

$^3/_4$ cup zbożowa extract *(see above)*

4 tablespoons sugar

$^1/_4$ ounce gelatine

1   Preheat the oven to 350°F.

2   Make the zbożowa extract: Put the zbożowa coffee and water into a saucepan and bring to the boil. Leave it to infuse, off the heat, for 15 minutes. Strain it and reserve.

3   Prepare the *succes* biscuit: whisk the egg whites, slowly adding the sugar as you do so, until they are stiff and glossy. Carefully whisk in the ground hazelnuts. On a sheet of greaseproof paper put a round form of 11 inches. Fill with $^1/_2$ inch of the hazelnut mixture. Pipe out the remaining mixture into thin fingers onto the surrounding area of greaseproof paper. Cook in the oven for 19 minutes. Allow to cool.

4   Prepare the *parfait*: In a heavy bottomed saucepan bring the water and sugar to the boil and boil until it reaches a temperature of 250°F. Meanwhile, whisk the egg whites until they hold strong peaks. When the caramel is ready pour it onto the egg whites, whisking all the time until it is well blended. Leave to cool to room temperature.

5   Beat the egg yolks lightly and stir in to the egg whites. Fold in the whipped cream and the zbożowa extract. Pour this onto the *succes* biscuit in its form. Smooth it out and freeze.

6   To make the sauce: heat the remaining zbożowa extract and dissolve the sugar and gelatine in it. Leave to cool.

7   Decorate the iced *parfait* with leftover crumbs from the *succes* biscuit and with the biscuit fingers.

8   Slice the parfait and arrange it on the plates accompanied by a little sauce. Serve the rest of the sauce separately.

Mille-feuille of white chocolate mousse with pink peppercorns and Pieprzówka vodka

MILLEFEUILLE DE CHOCOLAT BLANC, MOUSSE AU POIVRE ROSE ET VODKA PIEPRZÓWKA

For the white chocolate leaves

10 ounces white chocolate

$1/2$ teaspoon dry pink peppercorns

For the white chocolate mousse

9 ounces white chocolate

$1/2$ cup light cream

2 cups heavy cream

8 large egg whites

$1/2$ cup Pieprzówka vodka

1 teaspoon dry pink peppercorns, crushed

For the syrup

$1 \, 1/4$ cup water

5 tablespoons sugar

$1/2$ teaspoon dry pink peppercorns

4 tablespoons Pieprzówka vodka

For decoration

1 teaspoon dry pink peppercorns, crushed

4 tablespoons fresh mint

1   Make the chocolate leaves: break up the white chocolate and melt it in a *bain-marie* (see glossary) stirring from time to time. Leave it to cool down to 90°F. Cover a tray with plastic wrap and pour onto it seven extremely thin circles of cooled chocolate in decreasing size. The largest should be $2 \, 3/4$ inches and the smallest $3/4$ inch Crush the pink peppercorns and sprinkle the leaves of chocolate with them. Reserve.

2   Prepare the mousse: break up the white chocolate. Bring the light cream to the boil and pour it onto the white chocolate, stirring well until the chocolate has completely melted. Whip the heavy cream thoroughly. Whisk the egg whites until stiff. Gradually incorporate the cream into the chocolate mixture when it has reached room temperature. Add the vodka and then fold in the egg whites. Stir in the crushed pink peppers.

3   Make the syrup: boil the water with the sugar and the pink peppercorns. Cool until lukewarm and stir in the vodka.

4   Assemble the mille-feuille, placing the largest leaf of white chocolate at the bottom and working up in decreasing circles with a layer of white chocolate mousse sandwiched between each leaf.

5   Pour a little syrup onto a plate and stand the mille-feuille in the centre. Sprinkle a few pink peppercorns around it and decorate the plate with a little fresh mint.

Glossary

Bain-marie

A device to heat delicate ingredients which could be easily ruined by boiling. A pan is filled with water and placed over a gentle heat. Into this is suspended a bowl, which should not touch the water beneath it.

Bouquet garni

A bunch of herbs, often tied in a piece of muslin, used for flavouring, which is removed from the food before it is served. Traditionally made with a few sprigs of parsley, thyme, leeks and 1/2 a bay leaf.

Brown game stock

Makes 4 cups/1 quart

    4 pounds game bones

    1 pound *mirepoix* of vegetables (carrots, onions, celeriac)

    1 tablespoon tomato paste

    1 cup red wine

    1 *bouquet garni*

    salt

Brown the bones in a hot oven. Remove and put into a saucepan. Add the remaining ingredients and just cover with cold water. Bring to the boil, skim and leave to simmer for 2—3 hours.

Brown stock

As above but use chicken bones.

Brunoise

Diced vegetables of $1/8$ inch.

Clarified butter

This is necessary in some recipes. With the milk solids removed, the fat will be able to reach a higher temperature. You must only use the best quality unsalted butter. Melt the butter gently in a heavy saucepan. Allow to foam for a minute or two but not to burn. Remove from the heat and leave to settle for 30 minutes. Pour through a strainer lined with muslin into a bowl. The butter will be clear, the milk solids will remain in the muslin.

Coulis

A liquid purée made without flour.

Court bouillon

Used for poaching: makes 4 cups

    1 onion

    1 clove garlic

    1 carrot

    1 small piece celeriac

    1 bunch herbs

    1 small clove

    1 tablespoon vinegar

    salt, pepper

Put all ingredients in a pan add 4 cups of cold water, cover and simmer for at least 30 minutes. Strain.

Dandelion jelly

Makes 6 cups

    400 dandelion flowers

    $2/3$ cup orange juice

    $1/3$ cup lemon juice

    6 cups water

Put the above ingredients in a saucepan, cover and infuse for 70 minutes.

Add: 2 $1/2$ cups sugar, 2 $1/2$ ounces pectin.

Cook until it reaches a temperature of 226°F. Add a touch of lemon juice or citric acid.

Elderflower syrup

Makes 6 cups

    1 pound elderflowers

4 cups water

2 ½ cups sugar

Cook the above ingredients until a temperature of 226°F has been reached. Add a squeeze of lemon juice.

- **Flambé**

A method of coating food with alcohol which is then ignited.

- **Goujonettes**

Small strips of fish, cut into the thickness of a finger.

- **Granita**

A type of sorbet whose texture of ice crystals is slightly more granular than that of the standard sorbet and whose taste is less sweet.

- **Julienne**

Refers to the match-stick size strips which food, or in some cases flowers, are cut into.

- **Lemon & Olive oil dressing**

Olive oil, lemon juice (proportions of 6:1), salt and pepper whisked together.

- **Mirepoix**

Vegetables diced into ³/₄ inch.

- **Pithiviers**

A puff pastry dough used to encase a variety of fillings.

- **Sabayon**

The lightest base used for binding sauces and creams and is the foundation of several sauces in this book.

- **Salpicon**

Meat, fish, shellfish or vegetables cut into cubes of ¹/₂ inch.

- **Strudel dough**

Makes 1 pound

10 ounces white flour

³/₅ cup water

1 tablespoon oil

1 tablespoon white vinegar

salt

Knead until transparent, extend fully and rest on a damp cloth.

- **White chicken stock**

Makes 4 cups/1 quart

4 pounds chicken bones

1 onion, chopped

1 carrot, chopped

1 stalk of celery, chopped

1 *bouquet garni*

herbs

salt

To the bones add enough cold water to cover them. Add the remaining ingredients. Bring to the boil. Skim and simmer for 2—3 hours. Strain.

Index of dishes

Mille-feuille of white chocolate
mousse with pink peppercorns
and Pieprzówka vodka *136*

O

Opera of Warsaw *130*

P

Pan-fried Dublin Bay prawns
served in a crunchy cage
with a flower emulsion *22*

Pan-fried fillet of lamb served
with a juice of fresh coriander
and saffron kasza *104*

Pierogi of crab and bigos *24*

Pike fillet in a crust
of poppy seeds, served
with a nettle sauce *58*

R

Rhubarb and wild strawberry
sabayon, served with its
own sorbet *126*

Roasted veal shank flavoured
with savory and smoked
garlic *98*

S

Salad of smoked wild boar loin,
roasted curd cheese
and sweet and sour forest
blackberries *42*

Shortbread lily biscuits
with yoghurt sorbet *120*

Soup of sturgeon fins *46*

Steamed breast of chicken,
flavoured with blackcurrant
and peppermint *102*

Stew of veal tripe "Warsaw style" *40*

T

Tatry Mountain soup *52*

Thin slices of fresh
salmon trout flambéed
with Śliwowica vodka *28*

Turbot roasted with sunflower seeds,
served with a bison grass sauce *78*

U

Uszka of rabbit and marjoram,
served with a cumin
emulsion *38*

W

Warm gingerbread souffle,
served with a blood orange
coulis *122*

Warm salad of pike perch seasoned
with fresh herbs and slivers
of smoked eel *20*

Warm salad of venison fillet
marinated with pine honey *36*

Z

Zrazy of carp and crayfish,
served with a red wine
sauce, on a bed of vegetable
tagliatelle *68*

List of ilustrations

*I would like to thank Michael Goerdt for giving
me the opportunity to work in Poland. I would like to express
my gratitude to Patrick Lefranc and Paweł Oszczyk
of the Hotel Bristol and Joanna Puchalska for their help
in the preparation of this book.*